Memoirs of a Hospital Chaplain

Memoirs of a Hospital Chaplain

I Stand Near the Door

Chaplain Geralyn Cappabianca

ISBN: 151763458X
ISBN 13: 9781517634582
Library of Congress Control Number: 2015916437
CreateSpace Independent Publishing Platform
North Charleston, South Carolina

Published in the United States by Cappabianca Press, Southbury, CT

Contact: chaplaingeri@gmail.com

Facebook page: Chaplain Geri Cappabianca

Disclaimer

This book has been written and published strictly for informational purposes, and in no way should it be used as a substitute for consultation with healthcare professionals. You should not consider the educational material herein to be the practice of medicine or to replace consultation with a physician or other medical practitioner. The author and publisher are providing you with information so that you can choose, at your own risk, to act on that information. The author and publisher urge all readers to be aware of their health status and to consult health professionals.

The comments regarding spirituality and religion are solely the opinion of the author. They do not necessarily represent the teachings of the Roman Catholic Church or the views of the hospitals in which the author worked.

Dedication

This book is dedicated to my dear patients and their families. I am blessed to have been chosen to tell their stories. May they live on in our hearts and on these pages.

Acknowledgements

I would first like to acknowledge my daughter Jennifer Abbott-Cole who has been my strength and biggest fan. She read endless manuscript revisions, offered suggestions, and designed the cover and chapter dividers. She continues to encourage me to tell my story, that it *is* a story worth telling. I will be forever grateful for the gift of her love and presence in my life.

Thank you to my other editors Becky Tyre and Gail Altschwager. Without your help and gifted eyes, this first-time author would have been lost. Thanks to fellow published authors Clare Keating, Daniel Hazewski, and Margie Longano Miklas. Your encouragement and advice sustained me. Thank you, Jennifer Clement for your wonderful Foreword.

And finally, thank you to my chaplain colleagues who took the time to read and comment on the manuscript: Dennis McCann, Fr. Dan Kennelly, and Deacon Neil Culhane.

Table of Contents

Editor's Note

As the daughter of someone called to a spiritual profession I learned compassion early on. My mother, Chaplain Geri, is the embodiment of compassion; for her, it is as natural and necessary as breathing. When she came to me and said, "Jenny, I'm going to write a book about my experiences in the hospital," I knew that giving her stories to the world was yet another act of profound compassion. She could have kept them to herself, but instead she chose to share them knowing that many more people than she could physically reach in one lifetime would be comforted by them.

She will tell you—and she does—in the following pages that these stories don't belong to her and I guess that's mostly true. But as I read the manuscript and helped her to edit and craft the stories, I realized the thing they all have in common is HER and the compassion she showed to the people suffering in each one. She helped each person walk through a door that led to another part of their life, either here on Earth or in the great beyond; but for every one she stood at the door and said, "Do not be afraid."

Throughout my mom's writing process, I had the rare opportunity to witness her incredible growth as she walked through many doors of her own. When faced with her own humanity—her own grief—my mom persevered with extraordinary bravery. However, there were times she would become frustrated and say to me, "Is anyone going to want to read this?" Fear is a natural part of the creative process, of putting yourself out there; it was those times that I had the honor and privilege of standing at the door for her and saying, "Do not be afraid."

She has been described by her patients, colleagues and friends as an angel, a God-send, a ray of light, and spark of hope, all of which are true. She has a divine gift of allowing the spirit to live through her and she extends that spirit of compassion and love to all those who need it in an extraordinarily selfless way. As you read the following pages, know that her compassion and love is meant for you, too.

Jennifer S. Abbott-Cole, 2015

Foreword

At Saint Mary's Hospital, Chaplain Geri is our angel. There are certain professions situated on the "front lines" that bring life and death clearly into focus. Not only the hospital physicians and nurses who experience it daily, but all hospital personnel find that life and death are woven into the fabric of their work days at one point or another. Geri's role of Hospital Chaplain is invaluable to the providers who are called upon to save a life, the hospital staff as a whole, and the patients and their family members. She is our angel, waiting in the wings.

Through the years, Geri has performed many functions as our hospital chaplain. We heard her reading the morning prayer over the loudspeaker when we started our day, and caught sight of her in the halls and various departments as she visited with patients, their family members, and our staff. If there was a person, a unit, a piece of new equipment to be blessed—Geri was there—holy water in hand.

In 2012, the hospital suffered a terrible loss when one of our young internal medicine physicians died suddenly. In a short time, he had a tremendous impact on our patients, staff and especially many of the young doctors who had come to Saint Mary's for their residency training. To honor his life we held a memorial service in our auditorium. I watched as some of the most respected members of our medical staff shed tears. There were no words for the loss we were experiencing together as a hospital family. Geri possesses a special gift for knowing just the right thing to say, even at the most difficult times. She led the assembly and shared with us a beautiful poem, which I am so happy to see included here in the pages of this book. Through this poem and her gentle words, she encouraged us not to let go of our feelings and our memories even though our dear friend and colleague was no longer in our sight.

Geri organized an annual memorial ceremony for all members of our hospital family who had passed during the year. She had a butterfly garden planted outside the main entrance of the hospital and at the end of the ceremony we released butterflies in memory of those we had lost. One year, the weather was unseasonably cold and rainy. When we opened the boxes, the butterflies refused to fly out. They stayed close together and would not stretch their wings, perhaps knowing it was not the right time to go. Geri decided that she would take the butterflies home with her that night. The next day, when the sun came out, she opened the boxes to see if the butterflies would take flight. They emerged from their boxes and many of them landed on her, covering her arms and her legs. I wish I could have witnessed that moment, and wonder if the butterflies knew instinctually, or perhaps spiritually, that they had found a safe place to rest before continuing on their journey.

In these chapters, Geri invites us to share her very personal experience on the front lines as a hospital chaplain. One of our Senior Leaders, Dr. Steve Schneider, has seen Geri work with patients. He says that she is a "profoundly spiritual person. She makes everybody feel comfortable no matter what their religious beliefs are. She's a real jewel for us to have at Saint Mary's, a source of light."

As we walk with Geri through the doors of the hospital, and life and death, we learn that by embracing faith and acceptance each of us has the opportunity to be an angel and help ease the journey for others as they make their way to the other side of grief. Thank you, Geri, for giving us the reassurance that no matter what we are facing, we never walk alone.

Jennifer Clement, Corporate Communications Specialist, Saint Mary's Hospital, 2015

Introduction

You are standing in front of a door. It looms before you. You don't know what is on the other side. You are scared, maybe even terrified.

You ask yourself, how can I ever open this door and walk through it? You know you must open the door.

You hesitate. You say a silent prayer.

Now imagine that a warm, loving person appears near you. This person says, "It's OK, this is your very own door, created just for you. I will be here to help you open it and I will walk through it with you. Take my hand. Don't be afraid. You aren't alone."

This is what hospital chaplains do. We stand near the door.

Hospitals are places where people come for transition. The sick enter our doors broken and leave healed. Parents come to birth their children. They enter as a family of two and leave as a family of three (or more)! The dying come to transition from this life to the next. They leave their physical bodies behind in exchange for a body made of light. No one remains unchanged after walking through the doors of the hospital.

As a hospital chaplain, I see the hospital not only as a building, but as a spiritual crossroad with many doors. I walk from the door of the children's unit on the fourth floor across the hall and enter the door to the hospice unit. I walk from the intensive care unit on the third floor through the door to the maternity unit. Life begins on one side of the door, terminal illness and death on the other. One universe on one side, a completely different universe on the other.

The opportunity for spiritual transformation is ever-present in the hospital. A chaplain helps patients and families find meaning and purpose in a life forever changed by life and death and all the transitions, the doors, in between.

I walked through thousands of doors in my ministry with chronically ill and dying patients and their families. My chaplain ministry, in three different hospitals, has been challenging and rewarding. I have served at St. Raphael's in New Haven, CT, St. Vincent's Behavioral Health (formerly Holbrook) in Westport, CT, and currently, Saint Mary's Hospital in Waterbury, CT. The common thread among them is that anyone who walks through the door of a hospital, no matter where it is, is suffering, sick, afraid and vulnerable. Even friends and family members have worries and concerns about walking through the door with their loved ones.

In the following pages, I will share some sacred moments through the stories of several courageous people, most of whom did not walk out the door of the hospital physically healed. They left their bodies behind and walked through the door to eternity, spiritually transformed.

All of these stories are true. In some cases, I have changed names and circumstances to protect the identity of patients who I could not find or who wished that their identity remain confidential. Others willingly gave me permission to tell their stories.

Keeping these patients alive in my heart is an honor. They continue to inspire all who read their stories. As I write, I feel their presence with me, a witness to a life well lived. They have all, in some way, changed me forever.

I will also be sharing my own personal spiritual journey and what led up to my ministry as a chaplain. God uses all of me, the wounds, the joy and the challenges, as I minister to and support those I serve. I become God's instrument of compassion and love. I walk with patients and their families through their doors and they walk with me through mine. Together we weave a beautiful tapestry, each of us becoming part of the life of another, if even for a brief moment.

It has been an honor and a privilege to walk with so many people at their most vulnerable moments, in sickness, suffering, death and grief. The doors to sickness and death teach us many lessons about how to live our lives if we can get over our fear long enough to walk through and experience what is on the other side. A chaplain can help.

I invite you to walk with me through these many doors, to reflect on the doors in your own life, and choose how you will walk through them. These are sacred doors all, the doors to your own soul, the doors to eternity.

Chapter 1

Led By The Spirit

I have always heard the whisper of Spirit, even as a child.

I was born in 1953 in Stamford, CT, the middle child between two brothers and the only daughter in my Italian American family. My mom was a nurse by profession. My dad owned a travel agency, Cappabianca Travel in Stamford. My grandfather established the agency in 1906 and passed it on to my father.

My dad was a workaholic. Every day he went to "the office," even on Sundays. My mom took care of us, a typical 1950's mom. Her caring and love sustained us, even without dad around.

My family lived right behind St. Cecilia's Church. We walked to church every Sunday. My brothers and I attended St. Cecilia's School, literally in our backyard. The church and school became an extension of my house and home, I spent so much time there.

I loved Catholic school. I loved hearing the nuns talk about the saints, especially the mystical ones, who saw and experienced God. Even at a young age, I wanted to experience God too.

Mom was part of the Altar Society, a group of women who took care of cleaning the altar and washing the altar linens. I went with Mom during the week to help. One of my earliest memories of being on the altar was vacuuming the long, red rug. One day

I turned off the vacuum and looked out at the empty church. I remember thinking that only priests and altar boys had this view during Mass. Women weren't allowed on the altar, except to clean.

I knew at that moment that I wanted to become a priest. I secretly offered Mass in my bedroom, rolling Wonder Bread into little balls for Communion. I was too young to understand that this would never be possible. In hindsight, I can see that the Spirit had other plans, and would be guiding me through other doors, and ways to serve God's people.

As I grew older, I became more active in the church myself, joining the choir, and playing guitar on Sundays for the first "Folk Masses" in the late 1960's.

God and I were great with each other. Every day I was growing closer to God, getting to know and see Him more. My prayers were often answered, proving in my young mind that God was always there listening to me.

Then, one Saturday morning in April 1968, my dad kissed me good-bye before going to the office for the day. I did not know that I would never see him alive again. I was 14 years old.

I remember running to the church that afternoon when Dad was in the hospital, begging God not to let my daddy die. Please God, don't let my daddy die.

4

He died later that night at St. Joseph Hospital of an aneurism. I never got to say good-bye. My prayer was not answered. My deepest and most desperate prayer was not answered.

The questioning began: Where was God? Why did He let my daddy die? I felt abandoned by God and Dad.

I was angry. My journey of grief had begun, although back then grief was not recognized as a journey or process, so there weren't any support services. Mom was given tranquilizers to help her. We kids had no real support, except family, who themselves were grieving. We needed help. We needed someone to care for us. Mom needed someone to care for her.

I became the caregiver, a role that I would play for almost 50 years.

My Mom and I, and my two brothers, went through some desperate times in the following years. Mom tried to take over the running of the travel agency. She had no business experience and knew nothing about running a thriving business. It was a disaster. She dealt with this by hiring a manager for the office, remarrying the following year and moving all of us to Canada, where she was born and where her new husband lived. When the marriage did not work out, we returned to Stamford the following year. I was just beginning my senior year in high school.

Upon our return, I became the "mom" to Mom and my brothers, doing the grocery shopping, making meals, and cleaning the house. In counseling terms, it's called "the parentified child." For me, this provided a distraction, an excuse to deny my feelings of abandonment and betrayal and I fell into a deep depression.

I continued to go through the motions of going to Sunday Mass, playing guitar for the folk Mass, yet still questioning God: Why did Dad die? What is life and death? Where do we go when we die? Who am I?

One Christmas, the nun in charge of music at the Church gave me a gift. It was a metal cross with a quote on the back from Isaiah: "I have called you by your name, you are mine."

I remember thinking, really? Does God really know I am here? Does He even care?

I felt that this may be a sign from God, that maybe God hasn't forgotten me. Maybe I'm called to do something special, something that will help others who are also suffering. The door to ministry was slowly opening.

Then that door burst open and I had a profound mystical experience.

It was a warm summer evening and I was spending some time with my friend Steve. While we sat in the car, the warm breeze softly enveloped us. We were talking about God and how Steve was given the gift of a mystical experience many years before. I listened.

All of a sudden, I heard a loud rush of wind, like the sound of jet engines on take-off or landing.

The next instant, I remember looking out at the outline of the trees silhouetted against the deep blue evening sky. My internal "sight" suddenly shifted, as if a sacred door had been opened to me. The message I received was this: We are One, all life is One.

God opened that door for me. God was not a specific Divine person or saint, and I did not have a visual experience, but I knew that it was God. God touched me and the door opened. I walked through the open door.

That holy instant changed me forever.

At the time, an image that came to mind was that of the twelve Apostles in the Upper Room when the Holy Spirit came upon them with a loud rush of wind. Their eyes and hearts were opened. So were mine.

I was transformed. My deep depression vanished as if someone grabbed me by the shirt collar and pulled me out of a deep, dark well.

Steve was amazed. He saw and heard nothing. He listened to me with an open mind and heart as I described my mystical moment. We talked for many hours after that, but we could not explain what or how it happened.

Steve was the only one who knew about my experience for many years.

After that night, I was compelled to find answers to the meaning of my experience. I began a personal interfaith search for understanding. The Spirit would guide me.

In the early '70's, I was invited by a friend to come and hear a holy man from India speak in Stamford at one of the churches. His name was Bawa Muhaiyaddeen and he was a Sufi sheik from the mystical branch of Islam. He spoke of The Divine as all loving and embracing. He said that the path to God is difficult, but that God helps us along the path. He spoke of his own mystical experiences with God, the angels and Holy Prophets. He echoed the truth that God is One, we are one, the insight that I had been given on that summer night.

It was a step in my journey. I listened, and learned. My question about what happened to me wasn't totally answered, but it was comforting to know that others around the world have had these mystical experiences and that God does touch us directly. I suddenly didn't feel alone.

During this time, I began working with teenagers through a program called Young Life. This national program introduces teens to Jesus and His love. I really enjoyed the kids, playing my guitar, singing with them, going on retreats to delve into Scripture and Jesus' love for us.

One of the Young Life leaders gave me a poem. It was written by Rev. Sam Shoemaker who was born in 1893. Another door opened for me. This poem is what inspired me to continue on my spiritual journey and still gives meaning to my ministry today. This is a shortened version; the full text can be found in the appendix.

I Stand by the Door
By Rev. Samuel Moor Shoemaker

I stand by the door.
I neither go too far in, nor stay too far out.
The door is the most important door in the world –
It is the door through which men walk when they find God.
There is no use my going way inside and staying there,
When so many are still outside and they, as much as I,
Crave to know where the door is. And all that so many ever find
Is only the wall where the door ought to be.
They creep along the wall like blind men,

With outstretched, groping hands,
Feeling for a door, knowing there must be a door,
Yet they never find it….
So I stand by the door.

The most tremendous thing in the world
Is for men to find that door – the door to God.
The most important thing that any man can do
Is to take hold of one of those blind, groping hands
And put it on the latch – the latch that only clicks
And opens to the man's own touch….

Nothing else matters compared to helping them find
it,
And open it, and walk in, and find Him….
So I stand by the door…

As for me, I shall take my old accustomed place,
Near enough to God to hear Him and know He is
there,
But not so far from men as not to hear them,
And remember they are there too.

Where? Outside the door –
Thousands of them. Millions of them.
But – more important for me –
One of them, two of them, ten of them.

Whose hands I am intended to put on the latch.
So I shall stand by the door and wait
For those who seek it....
So I stand by the door.

My work with teens would continue for the next 20 years, first as a Young Life leader, then youth director at St. Stephen's Episcopal Church in Ridgefield CT, and finally as a high school guidance counselor in Ridgefield, CT and Southbury, CT. All the while, I felt called by God to "stand by the door" for teens, helping them through their difficult years as I continued to heal my own teen years. Little did I know that this poem would continue to inspire me through my chaplaincy as well.

In 1979, I married Steve. He was the one who was with me when I had my mystical experience. We were married for 23 years. Together we had two beautiful daughters, Jenny and Amy, both of whom are very spiritual. I am so proud of them.

Steve and I both had difficult times growing up and we each coped with this in our own way. Over time, we became more distant, the years of abuse and addictions in our family of origin eventually caught up with us, even though we went to counseling together for many years. We ultimately divorced in 2003, to go our separate ways, to try to heal.

Another loss, another grieving process. Another door.

During this time, I began to feel restless in my job as a guidance counselor. My position in the high school was more about scheduling and college applications, and less about working with teens through their life challenges. I felt that God was calling me somewhere else. I didn't know where, but I heard the call.

I left the high school. I trusted that God would reveal my next step.

A few months later, God showed me the way and opened a door. A dear friend, who was an Episcopal priest and chaplain at St. Raphael's Hospital in New Haven, invited me to come for lunch. She knew I was going through a difficult divorce and needed a job. She mentioned that I might be interested in applying for their Clinical Pastoral Education program, the training program for hospital chaplains. She said that I may not want to become a chaplain, but the year might help me discern where God was calling me next. It could be a time of exploration and healing.

I applied and was accepted for their yearlong residency program.

My spiritual questions remained in the back of my mind, nudging me to keep searching for answers. I was in another dark place after my divorce and I longed to see and feel the presence of God again.

God answered my prayer. I met another holy person from India. Her name was Shri Anandi Ma, teacher of Maha Kundalini Yoga. She came to the Woodbury Yoga Center in the summer of 2002, right before my chaplaincy training began. I had just completed a 6-week meditation course at the Yoga Center. The course, and meeting Anandi Ma, would change my spiritual view of everything.

Anandi Ma taught about a mystical branch of Hinduism that stressed the importance of going within to receive guidance and answers about life. She spoke about the kundalini, the spiritual energy of God that is within each of us, and that meditation helps us to get in touch with this energy. She offered an answer to my question about what happened to me.

She said that perhaps God had awakened this deep spiritual energy within, giving me the ability to understand the universal connection between every being. She explained that many ordinary people have these mystical experiences, and that the Hindu tradition has recognized this for centuries. Meditation, the quieting of the mind and going within, is the key to spiritual growth.

Another door.

This revelation rang so true for me. I finally felt that I had found an answer and a body of knowledge in the Hindu tradition that addressed many of my questions about life, death, and why we are here on this planet. She said that the answers to all my questions are within me.

It is amazing to me that all this happened just as I was about to enter chaplaincy training. As God would have it, all my searching came together that year. My chaplaincy training would be about becoming an interfaith chaplain. I learned how to respect all religious and spiritual traditions. Each person has their own path to God, entering through their own unique doors. I learned to honor their path, and walk alongside them.

We are One: all paths lead to God.

As I look back on my life and its many twists, turns, joys and sorrows, I can clearly see God's plan for me. Each experience helped me to grow closer to God, and closer to the people whom I am intended to help. It is a Divine plan, a tapestry of glorious colors and design. I am very blessed to see this in my own life, and I am blessed to be able to help others to see this in their own lives.

So as we begin our journey together, I invite you see with my eyes, feel with my heart, and walk in my shoes through the doors of the hospital.

My Chaplaincy Door

Clinical Pastoral Education is the training for hospital chaplains. After earning a Master's Degree in Divinity or a related field, one embarks on a yearlong residency in a hospital that offers this training. It is very much like a medical residency, with countless hours on call, attendance at all deaths, traumas, codes (emergencies in the hospital), and visiting patients and families to offer emotional and spiritual support while in the hospital.

I came to the chaplaincy program at St. Raphael's Hospital in New Haven, CT, in August of 2002 with joy in my heart, and I looked forward to beginning the program, a new door. I had a Master's Degree in Counseling and many years of experience as a youth minister and a high school guidance counselor. I was excited about chaplaincy. However, I was not prepared for what lay ahead. I did not know that I was staring straight at a terrifying door.

It was a Friday in September 2002, the first month of my chaplain residency. It had been an intense week. The process group meetings, study groups, 60 to 90 hour weeks, and writing "verbatims" (the interactions of the chaplain with a patient) was too much. My peer group consisted of four other chaplains who were not getting along. I was actually thinking of leaving the program.

That Friday night was my first on-call to cover the 500-bed hospital all alone because all the other chaplains had gone home. I told myself it would be a quiet night; maybe the pager would not go off.

My first lesson: there are no quiet nights in a hospital. The pager went off.

The surgical resident called me to the bedside of a patient in the Intensive Care Unit. Peggy (not her real name) had surgery earlier in the day and did not wake up from the anesthesia. The doctors tried everything and they didn't know what else to do. The resident asked me to speak with the son to prepare him for the possibility that Peggy might not wake up, that she might die.

When I arrived, I saw a young man, clearly distraught, at the foot of the bed. Even though I knew what the surgical resident told me, I asked Peggy's son what happened. I always like to listen to the point of view of the patient or family member as well.

"My mom didn't wake up after surgery. This wasn't supposed to happen, it was a simple surgery."

He was scared and angry.

Being a new chaplain, I said a silent prayer. I had no clue what to do or say.

"Is Peggy a spiritual person?" I finally asked.

"Yes, she is a Christian and attends a Protestant Church and studies the Bible regularly."

"Will you pray with me and Peggy?" I asked.

"OK, if you think it will help. I don't know what else to do."

I whispered in her ear, "Peggy, I am Chaplain Geri. Your son and I are going to pray with you."

I took his hand, and Peggy's hand, and we began to say the Lord's Prayer very slowly.

About half way through, Peggy's lips started moving. In small whispers, she began reciting the words along with us. "For the Kingdom, the Power and the Glory are Yours, now and forever, Amen."

I was amazed! So was her son! We looked at each other in disbelief.

After that, she began to moan, and we said the prayer again. This time she recited the whole prayer with us.

I stayed a little while with Peggy's son while she slowly began to respond. I then went out to see the surgical resident and told him what happened. He was so relieved. They had not been able to get any response from Peggy all day.

As I was leaving, over his shoulder, he said to me, "Please thank the Man upstairs for me."

Coincidence? Miracle? Door?

I went back to see Peggy on Monday morning. She was sitting in the chair, brushing her very long salt-and-pepper hair. It was gleaming as the light shone through it.

"You look wonderful!" I exclaimed. "You had us all very worried on Friday when you weren't waking up after your surgery."

Peggy smiled and took it all in stride, wondering what all the fuss was about.

I shared this story in my CPE group on Monday. We were all amazed and thankful that Peggy came back to us but we just couldn't make sense of it. We decided that it was a miracle and that it just wasn't her time to open her door, the door to her next life.

For me, this was an invitation to walk through my own door. I stood before the door the first day of the program with excitement and joy. Now, the door had been opened a bit wider and I was thinking of leaving the program.

Did this "miracle" happen for me as well as Peggy? I was at the threshold of the door to my chaplaincy. God was asking if I wanted to go all the way in. I had a new view of what lay ahead. Was I willing to take this on? Was I willing to walk with people through their doors? Was I strong enough? Courageous enough?

The answer was no. I wasn't strong enough alone. I knew that a Higher Power was at work here; call it God, or the Universe, or in my case, the Spirit. This was my door. God was with me. I had support from my fellow chaplain residents, my supervisor, and my family. I wasn't alone.

I walked through the door.

The Chaplain Resident

It was a very rocky year.

More than once, I asked myself what I had gotten into. On one occasion, about halfway through the program, I actually did leave the program when the going got really tough. My supervisor finally convinced me to return, that I could be a good chaplain, that this was all part of the process. Being in a hospital ten hours a day, seeing sickness, death, suffering and trauma, was very hard. I was still dealing with my own issues regarding death, dying, and living.

That year I went through a divorce, had a very bad car accident, turned 50 and grieved my father's death 36 years earlier. Yes, it was a very rocky year.

The Clinical Pastoral Education program is ultimately about helping others. First, the focus is on the chaplain's personal process. What do we, as budding chaplains, have inside of us that needs to be healed? Where and what are our wounds? Through our process groups and sharing our patient visits through "verbatims," we work on our feelings, our reactions, our faith in God, and our fears of death and grief. We affectionately call ourselves "wounded healers." This is of utmost importance when helping others. Our fears and issues must be addressed so we can authentically walk with others through their own processes. A person cannot be a chaplain and remain unchanged by what he/she sees, feels and experiences. For me, my worldview, my values, all that I held dear, changed forever. My own personal journey is an important resource to help me walk with patients and their families through their own doors.

I keep in mind that everyone is unique and walks in very different ways through the doors of suffering, grief, death, beliefs about God, the afterlife and regrets. I need to honor each person's road without judgment. The events in our lives unfold for a reason. They offer us many opportunities to learn compassion, acceptance, forgiveness of self and others. The lessons are endless. Every moment we choose the door.

Chapter 2

Sara

I met Sara (not her real name) a few years ago during one of her many admissions to the hospital and she shared her life stories with me. As a result, we became friends.

Sara was wheelchair bound with an oxygen tank and a "wound vac" strapped to the back of her chair to heal her bedsores. She couldn't move herself and she needed to be turned over in bed and carried to the bathroom.

She had lung cancer that spread to the rest of her body. She was paralyzed and in chronic pain. Her sad eyes peeped out from under her wig. She was still beautiful despite her illness.

One day I went to see her. She struggled to breathe. I saw a deep sadness on her face. She knew she was dying.

"What should I do, Geri?" she asked me. "Is there a heaven? Is there a life after this one?"

"I believe there is," I said.

"How do you know?" she asked.

"I've had experiences and felt the presence of people who have died. They are right here with us. I know there is life after this one, our spirits are eternal."

Sara nods and begins to pour out her heart.

"You know, I've been so unhappy for much of my life. I love my husband, but from the very beginning of our relationship, he was distant. He liked watching TV instead of being with me. We have a wonderful daughter together and for that I am thankful. And I have a beautiful granddaughter who is the love of my life. She gives me so much joy. I don't want to leave her, but I know I'm dying. I have so many regrets, so many things I still want to do. I used to be a ballroom dance instructor, you know. And look at me now. I can't even get out of bed myself; I have to rely on people to carry me. I hate to be a burden to anyone."

At this moment, her husband comes in.

"Hello, darling. I brought you some soup."

I watched as he began to feed Sara, a spoonful at a time. I felt tears stinging my eyes. I was so sad about her regrets about her marriage, that I wished she could talk with her husband about her many conflicting feelings before she died. I wished for more time for her to finish this unfinished business. I made a mental note to myself that this would be the topic of our next conversation if she would like to address it. I said good-bye to both of them and left with a very heavy heart.

At the time, I did not know that I would never have that conversation with Sara. She was discharged from the hospital a few days later, only to be re-admitted the following weekend when I wasn't there. She died that Saturday night.

I don't know if Sara finally found peace in her last hours, if she forgave herself and her loved ones for the choices they made. I can only hope and pray that she was surrounded by her family, whom I believe loved her very much. I hope that she was able to feel peace at her last moments. I know that she was welcomed by God with love and acceptance through the door of death, her final transition.

Is There A Heaven?

I tell this story because Sara asked me an important question about heaven. Does such a place exist?

Medieval painters gave us some magnificent pictures of heaven up in the clouds, but I believe that heaven is not a place far off in the sky. Heaven is right here if only we would be aware enough to experience it. Our loved ones who have crossed over are right here, still loving us, caring for us and protecting us.

Many family members have told me stories of their loved ones leaving little clues for them after they died. They find pennies "from Heaven" at stressful times, as evidence that their loved ones are here watching over them. Others have actually seen a loved one appear at the foot of the bed or sitting beside them on the couch. Some have vivid dreams, or feel their protective presence while narrowly avoiding an accident. Other common experiences are the whiff of perfume, a favorite song on the radio, the "knowing" they are there.

The door that divides heaven from earth is thin and getting thinner. Some even say that heaven is a state of mind; change your mind about what you see and heaven will appear.

We are spiritual beings having an earthly experience. As we evolve, we can experience heaven more and more right here. The eternal "now" is here for all of us if we will only open our eyes and hearts to the many miracles and wonders that happen every day of our lives and find the courage to walk through the door.

Chapter 3

Arthur

iane, one of my colleagues, asked me to come to her office early one winter morning. With tears in her eyes she said, "My dad is in the Critical Care Unit. Can you go see him? I'm so worried about him. He's not religious, but I'd feel better if you went to see him."

"Of course," I said.

I went right away. He was awake, which was unusual for a patient on CCU. Patients are often on the respirator or heavily sedated.

"Hi, Mr. G," I said. "My name is Chaplain Geri and I just came to say hello".

"Hi, Chaplain Geri," he said to me. "I'm an atheist! But I'm happy you came to see me".

"I'm happy to see you too. How do you feel?"

"With my hands!" he said with a silly smile. I knew we would hit it off right away.

"Diane asked me to come up to see you. She's very worried about you."

"I know," he said. "She worries about me a lot. I love her so much. But I am feeling better."

Arthur came to the hospital for breathing problems which would be the first of several visits for this problem during the course of the next few months. Arthur battled cancer several years before, and now it was back. His heart was failing as well. He was 89 years old, and Diane was his only child.

It would be difficult for both of them when they had to say good-bye. During these few months, I had the privilege of getting to know Arthur and growing closer to my wonderful friend Diane.

Arthur's last admission to the hospital was in early May and he could barely breathe. The doctors told Diane that they could probably pull him through this time, but if he had another episode, he might not make it. Arthur and Diane needed to talk about whether they wanted to continue treatment or allow the dying process to proceed. He would never recover from the spread of the cancer and he would be suffering as his bodily systems failed. They were suddenly in front of the door.

Diane called me down to her office again.

"We talked," she said. "He doesn't want any further treatment and he has suffered enough. I want you to talk to him about being ready to die. I don't know what he is thinking; maybe he's afraid. I know he's not religious, but I know you can talk to him about this. He won't talk to me. I just want him to be OK."

"I'd be honored to talk to him but he may not want to talk to me. It's funny; he told me he was an atheist, and when another chaplain went in to see him, he said he was 'Brother Arthur'. Then when the priest went in to see him, he said he was Catholic and the priest gave him the Sacrament of the Sick. Go figure!"

"Wow," Diane said. "I had no idea!"

A few days later Diane was going through some of Arthur's papers and found his Baptismal certificate. It was written in Hungarian and it came from a small Catholic church in central Europe 89 years ago. Diane never knew that her dad was baptized Catholic, he never told her. But he remembered, which was probably why he allowed the priest to give him the Sacrament of the Sick.

I went to talk to Arthur….about the door.

After chatting about the food, the nurses and how noisy the floor was the previous night, I began the difficult conversation.

"Diane told me that the cancer has spread and you don't want any further treatment. Do you feel ready to go?"

"Yes, I do. You know, I was a radar mechanic in the Army during World War II. I never got overseas. I was just stateside all the time, no big deal. My brothers saw action in Europe; they are the real heroes. But they're gone now. My two wives are gone, too. I'm not afraid. I am afraid to leave Diane, though. She'll have no one."

"She'll have us, her family at the hospital, and she has lots of friends to help her. We'll take good care of her," I said.

"Thanks, but she won't have me," Arthur said sadly. We both sat quietly for a few minutes.

"What do you think happens after we die?" I asked finally.

"Nothing. I think we just go to sleep and that's OK with me," he said.

"Well, if you find out that there is something after, like seeing your brothers and wives again, or being able to take care of Diane and help her from the other side, will you come back and tell me?" I asked with a smile.

"You'll be the first to know," he said with a giggle.

I knew that Arthur was going to be okay.

Arthur died the day before Memorial Day, very fitting for the humble radar mechanic who, through his work, probably saved many lives during the war.

I was honored when Diane asked me to conduct Arthur's funeral. We travelled to the National Cemetery on Long Island where Diane's mom was already laid to rest 30 years before. The Honor Guard played Taps, folded the flag, knelt down and tenderly and sweetly presented it to Diane and thanked her for her father's life in honor of the Country. We read emails from friends who couldn't come to the funeral, warm, funny memories of this remarkable man who changed so many lives just by being who he was.

The only religious part of the funeral was when we were placing the ashes in the grave. At that moment, as I was saying prayers, a big gust of wind came up and blew the big bouquet of flowers clear across the grass. It distracted us all at a very solemn moment. Knowing Arthur's sense of humor, I'm sure it was his way of letting me know that there *is* something after we die. He did promise that I'd be the first to know! He was also saying, "Don't bother with the prayers, I'm an atheist!" We all laughed and cried at the same time as we said goodbye, as Arthur walked through the door.

Letting Go

It is so difficult for families to let their loved ones go. Even if they have been sick and suffering for a long time, when the moment comes for their last breath, it is still a shock. The survivors are never ready. Diane and her dad were lucky to have had a chance to talk about what medical interventions he did or did not want, and that Arthur was awake and aware and could make his own decisions until the end. Diane honored his wishes even though it was hard for her to let him go.

Diane shared with me how she and her father came to have that difficult talk about the end of life and signing the Living Will papers. It took place many years before he actually died.

Diane, knowing that her dad was aging, and knowing that it was just the two of them, sought out a probate lawyer. He helped them write the Living Will, sometimes called Advance Directives, a legal document that specifies what medical interventions the patient wants at the end of life, such as using the respirator, artificial nutrition and hydration, and other means to keep him alive. After talking about what they did or did not want regarding medical intervention at the end of life, the lawyer drew up the papers.

However, Arthur still needed to sign them. The papers sat on his kitchen table for months and months and, as his health continued to decline, Diane kept reminding him to sign. She didn't know why he was hesitating.

Fortunately, Diane's Uncle Jon from Missouri came to visit the family before Arthur became really sick. Diane asked him to talk to Arthur about signing the papers.

Uncle Jon spoke with Arthur and found out what the delay was. Arthur didn't want Diane, his only child, to be burdened with making these difficult decisions, to remove life support, or to allow him to die naturally. Uncle Jon said, "Artie, you will be making it easier for Diane by signing these forms, not harder. You don't want her to go through what you and she went through when your wife died, do you?" Diane's mother died very suddenly, with no will or power of attorney. Diane remembers going to the bank the next day with her father and waiting in the parking lot until the bank opened. They needed to withdraw money and clean out the safe-deposit box before the bank found out her mother had died the night before. It was terrifying for Diane because she was only 21 at the time.

With Uncle Jon's help, Arthur finally understood. Out of love for Diane, he signed the papers. In the end, it did make it easier for Diane to make the difficult, final decisions for her father.

George: When Is Enough, Enough?

Diane was fortunate to know what her Dad wanted and was able to make decisions based upon his wishes. This is the ideal outcome of writing a living will.*

What happens when a family member disagrees with their loved one's wishes?

George (not his real name) was in his late eighties and had been suffering from many health problems for a long time. He had an underlying health condition that was terminal. He was in the intensive care unit for weeks and still the doctors were trying new interventions to try to keep him alive. He was a full code, which means that if he stopped breathing or his heart stopped, the medical staff would do everything to bring him back, including CPR, which can mean pounding on his chest to restart his heart. CPR can cause broken bones and punctured lungs from which an elderly, sick person may not recover. Sometimes the patient dies despite all these interventions.

I started wondering what was going on. I walked by his room day after day only to see George still lying there, unresponsive and on a breathing machine, with no improvement. The doctors said that George would probably not recover to the point where he could function without the respirator. His terminal condition would eventually take his life. George did have a living will in which he stated that he did not want to be kept alive on machines when all other interventions would be futile. Our obligation, as medical professionals, is to honor the patient's wishes.

The problem was that one of George's family members disagreed with him. His son was very religious and felt that the respirator should not be removed. One of our chaplains spent quite a bit of time with him, explaining that in the Catholic tradition it is okay to remove the respirator if all further medical intervention would not help him to recover. Further suffering would be caused by not removing the respirator.

Modern technology makes these decisions very difficult for family members because it appears to them that the family "pulled the plug," when in fact, the underlying terminal condition is the cause of death. In these cases, the machine gets in the way of the person returning to God.

The son wished for time to pray about the decision. A few more days went by.

At long last, the son agreed to let the respirator be removed and to let nature take its course. He later told us that the Holy Spirit had spoken to him and reminded him of the fifth Commandment "honor thy father and mother". His faith had provided him comfort and a way to let God take his father home. His father died peacefully soon after the respirator was removed.

It is so very important that families talk about a living will. The last few minutes of life are not the time to be asking, "Do you want everything done, or nothing done?" It is hard on the families and causes so much suffering for the patient.

Gather as a family to talk about your last wishes. Appoint a healthcare proxy in case you aren't able to make decisions for yourself or become unable to communicate. This person must be able to make these hard decisions based on what you want, not what the rest of the family wants.

Most states have a Living Will form on the state government website. Many hospitals have these forms available for you. In my hospital, either the chaplain or the social worker can bring a copy to patients and families and explain the process of signing. These forms can be signed without a lawyer, but must be witnessed.

Writing a Living Will or Advance Directives, and talking with your family about your wishes is one of the greatest gifts you can give. It really helps family members to honor your wishes and not what others may want for you. It is also a tremendous help to your healthcare professionals to know what you, the patient, want us to do for you. So please do this for you and your family. I have done it for mine. When the time comes, and you have these documents already at hand, you will be very glad you took the time to give this precious gift to your loved ones.

Chapter 4

Baby Gabriel

One otherwise quiet Monday morning, Sue, one of our social workers came to me and said, "We need to bury a baby. Will you say some prayers at the cemetery?"

This little one, a stillborn baby boy, was left in our morgue for two weeks. The family had originally said that they would come for him and bury him, but he was still here. Finally, after Sue contacted the family several times, the mother decided to turn custody of the baby, and responsibility of burial, over to us, the hospital. After the legal custody issues were resolved, Sue contacted a local funeral home who would help us to bury the baby.

It was the morning of the burial and I was trying to find the right words to say to honor our little one. I wanted to give him a name. This baby was surely an angel. Why not name him Gabriel, after one of the most well known angels in the Bible?

As I met the funeral director at the cemetery that cold, cloudy day in April, I prayed the following prayer:

Loving Jesus, you gathered the little children into Your arms and blessed them. Welcome our little angel Gabriel into heaven where he will be safe with You forever. May he rest in Your loving arms and be at peace, and may he await the day when we all will be reunited again.

Loving God, gently touch the grieving hearts of Gabriel's parents. Bring light to their path that seems so full of darkness in their grief. Bestow Your grace, strength and courage upon them so that they may once again walk in hope and love, when every tear will be wiped away.

May God bless the parents of little Baby Gabriel and all parents of all children who have died before life. Amen.

Why?

Grief over the loss of a child is perhaps the hardest loss to bear. Parents are not supposed to bury their children, our children are supposed to bury us. Many families can't handle such a tragedy and it can break them apart. They come into the hospital expecting to bring a healthy baby home, only to learn they will be burying their baby instead. No one can describe the emptiness, despair and questioning that follow this event.

Some parents try to forget that the miscarriage ever happened. They try again to get pregnant, sometimes with success, sometimes not. The loss is always there. I encourage parents not to bury this pain because it isn't healthy. The grief will come out in other unhealthy ways, like extreme attachment to the next child, hyper-anxiety over the health of the baby, or fear that the new baby may die too.

It is much healthier to grieve, to remember, to save the pictures and footprints and the tiny gown that some hospitals give to parents. They might choose to join one of the many support groups for parents who have lost a child. This baby was real, will always be their child, and needs to be remembered and honored.

Perhaps the parents of Baby Gabriel just could not handle burying their child. Perhaps money for the burial was not available, although our hospital and our local funeral homes are very generous in helping families at this most heartbreaking time.

These losses affect the hospital staff as well. I spend time with the nurses who deliver the baby and who support the mom in recovery. The doctors grieve too, and they may just need a hug after losing a baby. We all cry together. It is one of life's deepest mysteries, why babies die. None of us really knows why this happens, and sometimes even autopsies fail to pinpoint a cause.

It happened in my family as well.

In 1982, I became pregnant with my first daughter four months after my brother Frank and my sister-in-law Linda became pregnant with their first. It was so much fun to be pregnant together. Neither one of us knew the sex of our babies, we just knew that they would grow up together.

My family got the call in March of 1983, a few days before Linda's due date. The baby had stopped moving and the doctors were worried that something was wrong. We all prayed and hoped, but the baby had died in utero. The umbilical cord had wrapped around her neck, taking her tiny life in an instant. When Michelle, my niece, was at last delivered, she was beautiful, with curly black hair.

All our hopes and dreams for our children growing up together were shattered.

I was still pregnant with my daughter Jennifer, who was born four months later. I felt so guilty to have had a healthy baby girl while Frank and Linda lost theirs. *Why?* Is it God's will? That still sounds so hollow to me, even though I know that we don't have control over birth and death. It's hard to accept, hard to walk through that terrifying door, to somehow find a way to continue living.

In the best case, eventually, families accept what life has thrown at us. That is just what Frank and Linda did. They went on to adopt a wonderful baby boy, who is now married with children of his own.

My niece Michelle will always have a special place in my heart. I sometimes tell her story to grieving parents to help comfort them and to let them know that even though their lives will never be the same, with time, love and support, they will heal.

Many people have asked me what happens to the baby's soul. My personal belief is that each of these little souls is with us always even if their bodies are not. They are angels to us, helping us and guiding us, comforting us and taking great delight in being remembered by our family members. Telling brothers and sisters who were born before or after is a way of honoring these little ones.

I take time to remember Michelle and all of our Littlest Angels. I light a candle, say a prayer, and acknowledge that they are with me. They are, and always will be, members of our families forever.

Chapter 5

Chaplain Loren

$\mathcal{G}$od surely blessed us when Chaplain Loren came to work here at Saint Mary's. Her dedication as a chaplain and her willingness to fully participate in the Pastoral Care Department and the life of the hospital was a joy. She was wonderful to work with, jumping in and helping whenever I needed her. She was taking care of me as manager of Pastoral Care, helping me to do the day-to-day things. She was preparing to write the copy for our Pastoral Care web page.

We talked about our kids, who were about the same ages. We talked about the Episcopal Church, the Catholic Church, and our chaplain residency, both of us graduating from the same residency program at St. Raphael's. She and her husband were in the process of looking for a house in this area to shorten her hour-long commute from Westchester County. We became very close in a short time.

Loren represented many "firsts" at the hospital, and she truly broke new ground. She was the first person I hired when I became the new manager of Pastoral Care and one of the only non-Catholic chaplains at the hospital in a long time. She was the first woman to wear the collar of an Episcopal Deacon in this Catholic hospital. In the Catholic tradition, only priests and deacons wear clerical collars. I remember discussing it with her, asking if she was ready to break new ground, if she felt comfortable wearing her collar. Wear it she did. The staff received her so well, welcoming her and helping her to find her way.

Loren was with me when we blessed the "Fleet" of new patient transport beds. Now this was a first for both of us! Later that month she and another chaplain blessed the daVinci surgical Robot, nicknamed "Surgio". Never before had we blessed so many "things".

She touched the lives of many of our patients, including my mom.

The night before Loren started her new job with us, I had to rush my mom to the emergency room to get a blood transfusion. Mom was failing slowly; she was in her late 80's now. Her health was declining. It was becoming harder for me to minister to patients at the hospital and then go home to help my mom as well. To my delight, I found that Loren would be a much-needed "chaplain to the chaplain", helping me to walk through my own doors.

As it turned out, Mom would not be ready to leave until the next morning, the morning that Loren was starting. I welcomed Loren, and brought her down to the emergency room to show her around. The first patient she saw was my mom. As I got the discharge papers from the nurse, Loren and Mom were chatting away. I will always be grateful for Loren's love, compassion and caring presence with Mom. She continued to bring comfort to all the patients she saw.

Just after Loren started, the Leadership Team initiated a Mission Committee. Since all of the nuns were now retired from the hospital, it would be up to all of us to live out the Mission that the founding nuns had originally adopted for the hospital over 100 years earlier.

Loren and I talked a lot about the hospital as a "Catholic" hospital. Just before the first Mission Committee meeting, Loren asked me, "What does it mean to be a Catholic hospital?" I asked her to please ask that question at the meeting. "Are you sure you want me to do that?" as if I should already know the answer. I said, "Sure!"

So she asked. There was dead silence and all heads turned toward me. "Why are you looking at me?" I said. We all laughed and filled 3 flip chart pages describing our Catholic identity that included chaplains, crosses in every room, morning prayer on the hospital-wide speaker, abiding by the Ethical and Religious Directives, and living our Mission. This discussion shaped the Mission Committee's work for many years. I am grateful that Loren had the courage to ask the question that no one else thought to ask.

Loren grew to love and be loved by all of us and we looked forward to a long and beautiful ministry together. We did not know that God had other plans.

A few months after Loren started work, she took several sick days, then a few weeks went by and she didn't come in at all. One day, Loren and her husband came in to see me. Loren had a recurrence of ovarian cancer that had been in remission. She was going to begin chemo that very day. I was shocked and saddened. I hoped that she would beat the cancer again. I prayed for Loren and her family.

A few weeks later, I received a call from Loren's husband. She was dying.

I went to see her in the hospital that night. She was on the respirator and unresponsive.

I took her hand and prayed. Then her family and friends joined me and we encircled her. We prayed for her recovery, and strength and courage for her loved ones. I knew in my heart that she heard us and was aware of our presence. I then stroked her hair, whispering in her ear that all of us at the hospital were praying for her. "I love you, Loren," I said and I left the hospital feeling that I may never see her again. Still, I prayed that she would make it. She had made it before, had battled cancer a few years ago and won. She would do it again. She was strong and courageous. She was only 50 years old. I placed her in God's hands.

I could not believe it when her husband called the next day to say she had died.

One of the most difficult things I had to do was to write the email to the staff telling them that our chaplain had died.

Sometimes even a chaplain needs a chaplain.

At her funeral service, there were so many people: bishops, deacons, priests, family, and so many friends. I cried and cried. Then, during the singing of the 23rd Psalm, I felt the most incredible presence. I felt "goose bumps", and cried even more deeply. Somehow, I knew that Loren was with me at that very moment. The chaplain had come to give the chaplain a hug, right there in the middle of her special day.

Sometimes even a chaplain needs a chaplain. The chaplain comes.

Loren never liked to be the center of attention. She would not want me to focus on the sadness of her death, but instead to look at the happiness I still have in my life. She would want me to look at others and appreciate what we have and what we hope to make better.

There was a memorial service for Loren at Saint Mary's shortly after she died. As I was writing the homily, I came across the most wonderful reflection by Canon Henry Scott Holland, which I quote here. I use it many times at other memorial services, and I find it gives so much comfort to those who grieve. It gives me great comfort as well.

Death is Nothing at All

Death is nothing at all, I have only slipped away into the next room.

I am I, and you are you.
Whatever we were to each other, that we are still.
Call me by my old familiar name,
Speak to me in the easy ways you always used.
Put no difference into your tone;
Wear no forced air of solemnity or sorrow.
Laugh as we always laughed at the little jokes we
enjoyed together.
Play, smile, think of me, pray for me.
Let my name be ever the household word that it
always was.
Let it be spoken without effect, without the ghost of
a shadow on it.
Life means all that it ever meant.
It is the same as it ever was; there is absolutely un-
broken continuity.
What is death but a negligible accident?
Why should I be out of mind because I am out of
sight?
I am waiting for you, for an interval, somewhere
very near, just around the corner.
All is well.

After Loren died, her husband told me that she said that working at Saint Mary's was her "dream job." Even while she was sick, she kept saying, "I have to get back to work!" Well, Loren, you will always be a chaplain to me. I will call on you when I need a hug, as only a chaplain can give. I know you will be here, helping me walk through my doors with courage, gentleness and compassion. May God bless you, always.

Why?

Grieving is hard work. It hits us hard. It can paralyze us. It is complicated. All the other losses in our lives come rushing back with the experience of a new loss.

Loren's death hit me very hard. I really missed her presence, her smile, her dry sense of humor and her stark honesty. She died so quickly that sometimes I cannot believe that she is really gone.

The day Loren died was the 42nd anniversary of my father's death, April 27. The loss of Loren was fresh. The loss of my Dad was fresh again, too.

In many ways, my chaplain ministry is my attempt to heal my own wounds. Chaplains are known as "wounded healers." A large part of my chaplain training involved dealing with my own losses so that I can help others to cope with theirs. I feel the pain as I walk with patients and families through a very difficult and heartbreaking time. Mine is a ministry of presence, to grieve right along with my patients and families.

When Dad died, I asked God many questions. I still ask those questions, and have added more: Why do we suffer and die? Why do some people get sick? Why did Loren die at the beginning of her dream job and not be able to live out her life to help so many people?

More questions, more doors. How do I continue my ministry amid the losses?

My trust in Spirit and the exploration of many different spiritual traditions has helped me to begin to formulate a fluid, ever-changing and growing personal context for death, illness and suffering. It helps me to minister to others every day.

I believe that when a person's mission in this life is done, we cross over. On the other side of the door, we have a mission too. We do not just "rest in peace" or go to a "better place." Our souls eternally seek to expand, grow and love. We watch over our loved ones, helping them, loving them. I know as well as I breathe that there is a Universal Plan for us all, and we are all connected. There are no accidents, no coincidences, and no "untimely deaths."

I read an interesting philosophy that proposes that we create, with God, a map of our lives before we are born into this body. We create a "Sacred Contract" with God that includes unique events and experiences that provide us the opportunity to grow and learn. These are specific lessons designed just for us, and this is what "God's will" really is. However, we do not know what the Sacred Contract is until it unfolds before us. Our reaction to what happens to us is the key. Continually working on our reactions to life, moving from judgment and blame to love and forgiveness, is the goal of our time on earth.

The reason I like this spiritual view of life is that it eliminates the idea of blame. If God and I planned my own life, there is no one to blame, not even myself. The plan is perfect in its design to provide for me many sacred opportunities. What am I to do then, when bad things happen to me, except to learn and grow with love?

It is tempting to blame others for the bad things that happen: the system, a spouse, children, God. The good news is that I, and all of us, have the power of choice in every sacred instant: free will. I can choose to be empowered instead of being the victim. I can choose forgiveness instead of blame. I can choose healthy habits instead of destructive ones. As I do this, and I look back on the seemingly bad events, I can see the blessings as well. If my dad had not died the way he did, I know that I would not have become a chaplain. Despite death's pain and ferocious wounds, there are blessings for all of us every day.

As I grow spiritually through my own life with its twists and turns, I am continually amazed at the synchronicities, even down to the apple I chose in the grocery store today. That apple is in my hand, soon to be in my stomach, feeding my every cell. That apple grew on a tree that held its leaves and branches up to the sun, to the rain, and deep into the earth. That apple was created just for me. Amazing.

I believe that all of life is connected and we are all part of a great tapestry that would not be complete without our very own thread called "me." We have a right to be here and a purpose on the planet that may be as simple as just being present in every sacred moment.

I am living every day as if my life depended on it, because it does.

Chapter 6

Maggie's Shawl

*M*ichael was only 26. He came into the hospital unresponsive due to a drug overdose. He was now on the respirator. It was the week before Easter.

Michael's mom, Maggie, was at his bedside every day, holding vigil, praying for a miracle, a response, an open eye, anything. I prayed and hoped with her. I had seen too many of these young people come in, and I knew the prognosis was very poor. I did everything I could to support Maggie over those terrible, long days.

It was Good Friday, and after 5 days there was no change in Michael's condition. As I gently knocked on the door to the room, an image struck me. Maggie is sitting at the foot of Michael's bed. Jesus' mother stood at the foot of the cross, both women watching the life of their sons slowly ebb away. One happened long ago, one is happening today.

I brought her a prayer shawl, knitted by the women at the Basilica of the Immaculate Conception. They donate the shawls to us so that we can give them to the sick and dying. Every stitch represents a prayer, so prayers surround the person wearing the shawl.

Michael's shawl was blue. I gently laid it on the bed, covering his feet and legs. The Miraculous Mary medal sparkled in the dim light of the Intensive Care room.

"You are like Mary, Jesus' mother, watching over your son," I said to her.

Maggie began to cry and started to talk to me about Michael's long history of addiction and failed attempts at rehab. Still, he was her son, she loved him and did not want to lose him. I held her hand and gave her a hug. There are no words, only tears, when feelings run so deep.

"Thank you for your care and concern, you have been a comfort to me this last week. The prayer shawl is beautiful," she said.

Michael died that weekend. I called Maggie and told her how sorry I was.

About a month later, I was called to the lobby of the hospital. Someone wanted to see me. It was Maggie, standing at the desk, with a big bag in her arms.

"I began making this when Michael died," Maggie said. "The prayer shawl you gave me brought me so much comfort that I wanted to make one for you to give to another patient who needs it."

I was so amazed that after all Maggie had been through, she still cared about easing someone else's suffering. She brought the shawl to the hospital herself, the place where she last saw her son. It must have been so difficult to come back.

"I will put this in a special place and give it to a special person," I assured Maggie. "Thank you so much, and may God bless you!" Maggie hurried out of the lobby doors. We were both fighting back tears.

A short time later, I was able to give the shawl to the mother of a young man who had been in a severe motorcycle accident, and was in critical condition. I told Maggie's story to the mom and gave her this very special shawl. Maggie's shawl must have been very special, because the young man recovered from his accident and he now keeps the shawl on his bed.

That was the first of several shawls that Maggie made. She brings one to the hospital every year on the anniversary of Michael's death. Just this past Easter, Maggie brought her shawl to me. She also brought a very special person with her, her one-year-old grandson. His middle name is Michael. Life goes on.

The strength and compassion that Maggie has inspires me every time I think of her and the loss of her son. There is nothing more painful than burying a child.

Addiction is an unforgiving disease. It not only affects the addict, but everyone around him/her. The devastation is monumental and often there is no help if the person cannot do what it takes to stay clean and sober.

In my experience working with detoxing patients, I have found many addicted persons to be very spiritual. They may have been through tragic events in their lives; they search for God and answers to life's many mysteries. Many have feelings that run deep. They may have underlying issues such as: anxiety, attention deficit disorder, clinical depression, bipolar disorder or schizophrenia. The addiction may be a form of self-medication. Obtaining a correct diagnosis and prescribing proper medication can help, along with counseling and a commitment to a 12-step program. It is a tough road.

Every parent worries about their children. When I see an overdose or a drunk driving case involving a young person coming into the hospital, and watch the devastated parents sitting at the bedside, I know that that parent could be me.

I am reminded that life is short, that telling my daughters that I love them every day is the most important thing I can say to them. I treasure the moments we have together, grateful for the love we have in our lives.

Maggie, with her shawls, is paying it forward. She continues to inspire me with her strength and courage. Her shawl blesses the person who receives her loving, prayerful, priceless gift, a gift made by a mother who has stood at the foot of the cross.

Chapter 7

The Wedding

" Sure we can do a wedding," I said to the hospice social worker who called me one sunny fall afternoon.

A wedding in a hospital? Yes, we have had many. This one was very special.

A 55-year-old woman with cancer was admitted to our in-patient hospice unit. Further medical interventions were futile and she had only a few weeks to live.

The cancer patient's daughter was planning a spring wedding. Mother and daughter both knew that Mom would not live to attend the wedding.

The Pastoral Care Team and the Hospice Team sprang into action and together we became wedding planners!

The hospice team arranged for a reception in the family room of the hospice unit. The bride and groom went to city hall to get the marriage license, and Pastoral Care ordered a cake from the best bakery in town. One of the hospice chaplains prepared to conduct the ceremony. She asked if she could use the Chapel, and the bride's mother would come down from the hospice unit in a wheelchair to attend.

Since Saint Mary's is a Catholic hospital, I needed to call the Archbishop to ask permission to do a non-Catholic wedding in the Chapel. After hearing the circumstances, the Archbishop gave his blessings to the couple and her mother, promising his prayers for them. They were deeply touched.

Next, the flowers. I love flowers! I was so happy to assist with this part of the event.

I asked the bride what she would like. She said she would like her head wreath, made of tiny artificial roses, adorned with fresh flowers. Very simple, she said.

I brought the wreath to my florist, and, after sharing the story with her and shedding a few tears together, the florist carefully wrapped the wreath with flowers, baby's breath and ribbons. It was beautiful. With funds donated from Pastoral Care, we bought corsages for the mothers, bouquets for the bride and maid of honor, boutonnieres for the groom and groomsmen. We were all set.

After I ordered the flowers, a dear friend of the bride sent flowers as well, so we had two of everything!

Is it possible to have too many flowers at a wedding? Not this one. There were plenty of flowers to go around, and the bride was so happy to have enough for everyone.

It was time for the ceremony to begin. The beautiful bride and groom came down to the Chapel. I hugged and kissed them. Her mom appeared, looking radiant, in the wheelchair, wearing the beautiful head wreath and holding the bouquet that I had made for the bride. The bride was wearing the head wreath and holding the bouquet sent to her by her dear friend. It was the most beautiful sight I have ever seen.

Everyone cries at weddings. The hospice staff and I stood at the back of the Chapel, watching with tears in our eyes.

The bride's mother died peacefully exactly one week later.

I received a precious thank you note from the bride and groom that I will treasure. It is such an honor and privilege to be a part of these life events, to help people to walk through the their doors to whatever awaits them on the other side. In the daughter's case, the door to married life. In the mother's case, the door to eternal life.

Chapter 8

Near Death

*O*ne of the most valuable tasks of chaplain training is called the "verbatim." It is a written word-for-word conversation with a patient with whom the chaplain has had a significant interaction. The verbatim is presented to the group of resident chaplain peers who critique it. We question the presenting chaplain about what he or she was feeling during the conversation, inviting reflection and introspection. This is for the benefit of personal growth, to help the chaplain resident to listen better and get to the core issue of concern for the patient. Needless to say, CPE is exceptionally challenging, life changing, and makes us more caring and compassionate chaplains.

As we chaplains continue to grow in our ministry after CPE, the verbatim remains a powerful tool for growth and feedback.

The following is a verbatim that I presented to my staff about a patient who had two Near Death Experiences (NDEs). Near Death Experiences* are some of my favorite stories from patients. Their experiences of the tunnel and the light, seeing their relatives, Jesus, God, and a total feeling of peace and bliss bring joy to my heart. As a person who has had mystical experiences myself, I do my best to affirm these patients who have had a glimpse of what is beyond the door.

The verbatim always begins with the background of the patient. "Bud" is not his real name.

Bud

His background: male, early 70s, recovering from a heart procedure.

The conversation:

Chaplain: Hi, I'm Chaplain Geri. I just came to say "Hi!"

Bud: (smiling) Hi, how are you?

Chaplain: I'm fine, thank you. How are you feeling?

Bud: I'm doing fine. I hope I might be going home on Friday.

Chaplain: That's great. (We chitchat). Do you have a particular faith or religion or belief? The computer says you are "not affiliated".

Bud: That's right. I don't want religion forced down my throat.

Chaplain: I agree.

Bud: But I'm a believer in my own way. Do you have a minute?

Chaplain: I certainly do. (I always know something is troubling the patient when they ask me "if I have a minute." As I pull up a chair, I am honored and ready to listen.)

Bud: I was in a mud hole in the war and I was very scared. I saw God. I told God that if He got me out of it I would be a good person. And He did. That was the first time I saw God. Then again, at this hospital, I died and I came back. I saw the light twice, but I'm still here.

Chaplain: (amazed) You saw the light? Twice? Wow, when did the second one happen?

Bud: September first.

Chaplain: Just a few months ago?

Bud: Yes.

Chaplain: I would love to hear all about it, if you are willing to tell me.

Bud: Sure. I was having angioplasty done, and I saw the light. I looked down and saw them working on my body. I guess my heart stopped. When I was young, when my mom got mad at me, I would go outside, climb a tree, and just sit there. It was so peaceful, the gentle wind blowing through the leaves. I was back in that tree again. I just wanted to stay there. I did not want to come back into my body.

Chaplain: Why did you come back?

Bud: They told me I had to, they were pinching me and prodding me, I had to come back, but I did not want to. Then I saw that they were using the paddles on me and shocking me and so I came back.

Chaplain: What an amazing experience. You are very blessed, especially to have had two of them.

Bud: Yes, I am. I know that I am here for a reason and that it is not time to go yet, but I know what is waiting for me when I get there. (Nurse comes in with a big red heart pillow that all the patients get after a heart procedure.)

Bud: I am so happy to get this; I have been waiting all day for it.

Chaplain: Yes, all our heart patients get them.

Bud: And I'm going to have everyone sign it. (appears very happy) Will you do me the honor to be the first to sign it?

Chaplain: I would be more than honored to sign it for you. What would you like me to write on it that will continue to inspire you?

Bud: Just what you said to me before about being blessed.

Chaplain writes: "To Bud, you are very blessed. Chaplain Geri"

Chaplain: I am going to tell you a little story about a heart. If you try to balance a heart on its tip, it falls over and breaks (chaplain demonstrates with the pillow). But if you balance it on the round parts with the tip pointing up, it is centered in God and it won't fall over and break (chaplain draws a heart next to her name on the pillow)

Bud: I really like that. Thank you so much.

Chaplain: You really know what it means to have your heart centered in God, and you are so blessed. I am so happy that I came in to see you.

Bud: I am very happy too. Thank you so much for coming in. Have a wonderful day!

Chaplain: Thank you. You too. I hope you have a speedy recovery and go home soon. God Bless!

Bud: Thank you. Bye!

The verbatim always ends with a spiritual reflection:

Bud was a very pleasant man who had two life changing experiences. There is a saying that "there are no atheists in foxholes." In Bud's case that was certainly true.

Even though he was not religious, or particularly spiritual, he was very clear that God touched him in both these experiences. He was a man who does not believe in religion, yet he knew God when he saw Him in that foxhole.

Bud was certainly a grateful person. He said that he was grateful for the good care here at the hospital. He was grateful to be alive. There was a peace about him.

I visited him again the next day and met his family. They were very happy that he was still with them. I am sure that they hope he stays a little longer until he sees the light again and is finally welcomed home.

This is the end of the verbatim.

Much discussion among my staff members followed. We talked about theology and the near death experience, and the current research and books being written about them. We stressed the need for chaplains to be non-judgmental and allow a safe and compassionate space for patients to discuss these intimate encounters with God, despite our own personal beliefs. It is sacred space and we are witness to a very private and intimate walk through the door with our patients who trust us enough to share this life-changing experience.

Jill

Jill (not her real name) was patient whom I saw on the Critical Care Unit. She came in for surgery but did not wake up as expected. She remained in a coma and on the respirator for two weeks. When she finally woke up, she told me an amazing story.

She said that she went to heaven and saw her husband and her mother-in-law both of whom had died many years before. Her husband looked just like he did when she first met him. She said she kept telling him how handsome he was. She had wonderful conversations with him during the near death time, as well as with her mother-in-law, with whom she was very close. She then said that she saw a big brown ball coming at her, and couldn't imagine what it was. When it finally arrived at her feet, it was her dog who had died several years before. They had a wonderful reunion. Who says that dogs don't go to heaven?

When she finally came out of the coma, she was at peace.

Before this experience, she had been afraid to die. Now she had no more fear.

She lived for several more months until she finally walked through the door, entered the light and stayed.

Carlos

Carlos, one of our staff members, worked on the 3 to 11 shift. One afternoon, he was supposed to be in one of our office buildings doing routine maintenance. Everyone else had gone home so he would have been there working alone. At the last minute, however, his assignment was changed to be in the main part of the hospital where there were many people around.

As he worked, he felt a gripping sensation in his chest. He passed out and fell to the ground. The next thing he heard was the voice of the emergency room doctor saying, "We got him back!" Carlos's heart had stopped. He woke up after an intense round of CPR to get his heart going again.

He later told me that while he was unresponsive, an amazing feeling of peace came over him. It began in his chest and flooded his body. It was indescribable. He was not afraid, and he knew that it was Jesus taking care of him. He did not want to wake up. He wanted, like many others who have been there, to stay in that warm, unconditionally loving embrace.

Carlos said that if he had been in the other building, he would have died. No one would have found him until much later that evening, or even the next morning. He knows how lucky he was. Even though he walked right up to death's door and peeked in, it was not his time to walk through. He came back.

Whenever Carlos and I see each other, usually right before I go home for the night, he has a big smile on his face. He reminds me of the day Jesus saved him, and I smile and remember too.

Carlos is grateful every day for his family and the time he is able to spend with them. He knows he was given a second chance at life and he says, with wonder in his eyes, that this experience changed his life forever.

Technology and the Near Death Experience

The medical field has changed significantly over the last 40 years. As we use more and more life-saving equipment to revive people after cardiac events and other traumas, many more people are reporting near death experiences. Many of them are similar: the tunnel, the white light, greeting a deceased family member, seeing Jesus or a being of light, or angels. They are told to return to finish out their life.

In the 1970s, Dr. Raymond Moody began researching Near Death Experiences. He documented these stories in his book, _Life After Life_. Since then, much additional research and documentation has been done to record these events. Many people, from physicians to young children, have written books about their experiences.

I remember attending a presentation given by Dr. Moody about his research shortly after my own mystical experience in the 1970's. I wondered if I might find an explanation about what happened to me. It didn't quite fit, but my fascination with the near death experience began and continues to this day.

Those who see what is on the other side of the door are changed forever. Some have trouble adjusting back to this earthly existence. They long for the unconditional love and peace that they experienced on the other side. They feel great loneliness because others do not understand what they saw and felt. Worst of all, some are judged as being crazy or having delusions brought on by the devil.

The question comes up if this experience was real, or was it the result of chemicals in the dying brain that causes the experience, as science proposes? The people who have shared their mystical or near death experience with me are totally convinced that for them, it was real. There is still no definitive scientific answer. The research continues.

Chemicals or not, the person who experiences a near death experience (NDE) or a spiritually transformative experience (STE) is changed forever as I was. We return with an expanded view of the meaning of life. We find purpose and direction for our lives. I certainly did.

I learned that it is very common for people to have near death experiences throughout history and all around the world. It is also common to avoid sharing them for fear of ridicule or judgment. So many patients say to me, "You're not going to believe this, but this is what happened to me." They share,

happy to feel acceptance and affirmation. I encourage them to find meaning in these encounters, to allow the changes in themselves to take hold, to follow
their now open hearts and minds. I encourage them
to keep the door open to this part of themselves, to
their very soul and God.

I feel honored when patients share these very
intimate and personal experiences with me. These
stories, as well as my own mystical experiences, re-
inforce my ministry with the sick and dying and their
families. I know that there is life after life and that our
spirits live forever. When our earthly job is done, we
leave the body and continue our journey. Life never
ends; it just changes. Another door, another opportunity to learn, to grow and to love.

*One of the best resources for anyone who has
had a near death experience (NDE) or a spiritually
transformative experience (STE) like I did, is the
International Association for Near Death Studies,
www.iands.org where you will find a wealth of information. There are many local groups all over the
world who meet to discuss their experiences and
support one another in a warm and welcoming way.
Their latest initiative is helping veterans who have
had an NDE cope with their experience and reinte-
grate into life.*

Chapter 9

John Doe

" Trauma alert, Emergency Room! Trauma alert, Emergency Room!" the overhead speaker trumpets. I am in the middle of approving time cards for the week, not a good time to have to run to the ER.

As always, I drop what I am doing. I save my work, grab my pad, pen and prayer book. My pager squawks and vibrates on my hip.

I hurry to the trauma room in the ER. Doctors, nurses, respiratory therapists, run past me. They always get there first.

I arrive. We are waiting for the patient. Near the door.

There are twenty staff members already there: medical and surgical residents, trauma nurses, x-ray techs, blood supply staff, and of course Pastoral Care. I stand near the door, praying for the patient, for the doctors, nurses, and the family.

I hear Lifestar, the medical helicopter, overhead as the ER doors open and close, letting in the frigid air. It is only 10 degrees outside and we don't yet know who is coming in. Is it a car crash, someone falling through the ice, shooting, stabbing, suicide attempt? It could be any of these.

The medical staff suits up with gowns, gloves and masks. I hang back, behind the nurses' station. I am not needed in the first few minutes of the trauma, except to pray, and stand near the door.

We wait. The tension is palpable. There is nervous laughter as someone cracks a joke.

Finally, the ER doors swing open as the gurney is wheeled in and the patient is taken to Trauma Room 2. Everyone springs into action. The Lifestar nurse and pilot brief the medical staff as they go to work. We all look to see if the EMT is doing CPR to re-start the heart. Thankfully, not this time.

The patient is awake, screaming, with his hands waving. It is a good sign; at least he is alive. We find out that it was a motor vehicle accident and there was a fatality at the scene. This driver was the lucky one.

The priest on-call arrives, having heard the overhead code. I tell him that it looks as if the patient is alive, but we do not know if he has a religion. No need for the Sacrament of the Sick yet. I promise to call him later after we learn more.

This patient is a John Doe, which means we don't know who he is. He came in from quite a distance, so no family has arrived yet to identify him. I leave word with the unit clerk to page me when the family comes, or when the patient is stable enough.

I went to see "John Doe" the next day. He now had a name, and his family was by his side. He was recovering on one of the medical floors with only minor injuries. He described the accident to me in detail: seeing the car coming directly at him (it was a head-on collision), feeling so helpless to get out of the way, and the sound of the Jaws of Life used to extricate him from the car. He was grateful to be alive, knowing it could so easily have been a different outcome. He felt so bad for the driver who died. He said an event like this really puts his life into perspective and vowed to remember how precious his life is.

The Emergency Room

The chaplain is part of the trauma team. My role in the trauma involves, at first, standing near the trauma room door praying for the patient. Then I wait.

I wait for family to come. After they arrive, I wait with them until the medical team has stabilized the patient enough to speak with them. I get coffee, tissues, water, call the priest for the Sacrament of the Sick or perhaps call their own pastor. Sometimes I run from the family room to the trauma room to give updates to the family on the status of the patient. I hold a hand, say a prayer, and give a hug. Then the moment arrives when the trauma doctor comes in to tell the family the fate of their loved one. Which door will this family walk through today? Death or life? Suffering for sure. Whatever it is, I will walk with them.

The chaplains, priests, ministers and other Pastoral Care staff play a vital role in the hospital, especially in the ER. My role as a chaplain in a trauma frees up the Emergency Room staff to care for the patient while I care for the family. After the trauma, I comfort and support the staff if they need it. If a child dies it is especially difficult. The staff really takes it hard. They do not have time to grieve, the next patient is usually on the doorstep waiting for help.

I deeply admire the ER staff; they have so much strength and courage to do what they do every day, hour after hour. I do whatever I can to help and support them by offering time to talk, giving hugs, telling them what a great job they do caring for our patients.

Together, we see patients and families at their worst times as we try to save lives. If we cannot, we help the family cope with the loss as best we can.

More Questions than Answers

As a chaplain I see and experience a lot. Many people say to me, "I could never do what you do." It is true that the chaplain is a unique character, carefully walking the fine line between dimensions of birth and death, religion and spirituality, incredible grief and deep peace. I stand by many doors with my patients, the most significant of which are the doors to birth and death. There are many different doors as well, the doors to healing, the doors to spiritual awakening, the doors to forgiveness.

The human body is miraculously strong and can recover from illnesses, traumas, and accidents. However, life is unpredictable, it can end in one moment, or change forever in the next. The outcome is not in our hands.

We all pass through these doors, the doors of transition, and the way we pass through them makes all the difference.

It is not what happens to us that ultimately matters; it is how we act and react to what happens to us that is the key. I have witnessed such strength and courage in patients and families as they face unimaginable adversity, despair and hopelessness. Many people's faith and beliefs can give them hope and peace in life's darkest hours. A family's love, caring and support can lift spirits and surround the patient with priceless affection. Some patients have no one, so the chaplain or a caring nurse or other care provider becomes their support and caring presence as long as they are with us. We do our best to provide what comfort we can: a prayer, holding a hand, giving a prayer shawl. No one should die alone, so we are there to walk with the patient through that final door.

Chapter 10

Newtown:
The Darkest Day

We waited. We watched. No one came.

Betty, the Chief Nursing Officer is looking for me. It is about 10 a.m. on Friday, December 14, 2012. It is a typical cold day in December at the hospital. Patients are getting ready for discharge; the Emergency Room is packed as usual. It is Advent, Christmas is right around the corner.

I finally catch up with Betty and she looks at me with horror in her eyes. "Pray. There's been a school shooting."

I follow her down to the Command Center across the parking lot. The Command Center is opened for a major crisis that involves either the entire hospital or the community.

Several senior leaders and security officers are already there. They called a silent "Code Triage," which means a mass casualty incident. It is a "silent" code because we do not have enough information to call a full code, which mobilizes the trauma teams in the hospital.

The TV is on, all eyes are glued to it. The tension in the room is off the charts.

A shooting. At Sandy Hook Elementary school in Newtown, CT., only a few miles away.

Hurried calls are made to the Emergency Room, Critical Care, and the blood bank, in case we needed to accept patients.

The Command Center was buzzing with plans as we prepared to help in this disaster. How many patients could we take?

For hours we wait, pray and hope, watching the reports on TV and getting information through our emergency resources.

Then we learn the horrifying truth. The children, their teachers and the shooter, were dead.

The few survivors were taken to another hospital. When it became clear that we would not be receiving anyone, we closed the Command Center with great sadness for everyone involved.

Word spread quickly around the hospital through the TVs in the lobby and in the patient's rooms. All the stations were covering the tragedy, so it did not take long for everyone to learn what had happened. Several staff members had children in the schools in Newtown. They swiftly left to try to find their little ones, while we all prayed that they would be OK.

Later that afternoon, I went on the overhead speaker and said a prayer for all those involved, for the children, their families, the school staff, the people of the town, the shooter and his mother. We wept.

The next week we held a Memorial Mass for the victims and their families. The Chapel was packed.

I preached this homily on that sad day:

"Then the wolf shall be a guest of the lamb and the leopard shall lie down with the kid; the calf and the young lion shall browse together with a little child to guide them. There shall be no more harm or ruin on all my holy mountain."

These are words from the prophet Isaiah. We spoke them only a few weeks ago in the Scripture reading at Mass at the beginning of Advent. We choose to speak them again today. These words predict a time of peace, a time of love between enemies, "Led by a little child."

Today we find ourselves struggling, grieving a loss that is beyond comprehension, at a loss for even the words to describe the depth of our sorrow. We are paralyzed and numb, angry and hopeless. Helpless. How can this happen? Why did this happen? We have all become victims of this violent act.

Yet, there has been such an outpouring of love, gifts, teddy bears, balloons, and therapy dogs visiting from Chicago. A man calls from across the country to a local coffee shop and pays for a cup of coffee for every Newtown resident. Amazing support pours in from all over the world, from the Pope to the Queen.

It is an amazing example of human kindness and compassion at its best in response to an act of humanity at its worst.

We do not have to remain victims, hopeless and helpless. We must not let these little children and their brave teachers die in vain. President Obama said in his talk on Sunday night, "What choice do we have?" Well, we *do* have a choice. We can choose to continue to be part of the darkness, numb to the little things we do every day that support it. Or we can keep this kind and compassionate part of our humanity growing, going so strong that it outshines the darkness. We always have a choice.

How can we do this? Nurture peaceful homes. Remove anger, hate and prejudice from our hearts. Remove the guns. Work to end domestic violence. Repair relationships with our friends and family members. Choose not to give gifts of violence—video games, war toys, toy guns. Choose not to go to movies that depict violence, sending a message to Hollywood and toy manufacturers. Turn off violent TV shows. Love more, listen more, and hug more. Teach our children peace by living peacefully ourselves.

I have a friend who is a retired school administrator. He told me that when a kindergarten class begins school for the first time, the class is known as the class of "such and such" year. This class would have been known as the "Class of 2024" if my math is correct. He said that this class will always be known as the class of the Sandy Hook school shooting and it will haunt them.

I'd like to think that this first grade class, these children, will not be remembered for the shooting so much, but as the class of children that lead the way to the beginning of a new and peaceful world, starting right here. The class that plants trees to remember their classmates, not seeds of hate; the class that reaches out to fellow classmates instead of bullying; the class that pays forward the kindness that was shown to them in their darkest days. This is what can change our society from a society of violence to a society of compassion and caring, where the lion can lie down with the lamb, led by the "little children". Then there will be no more harm and ruin on God's Holy Mountain.

Jesus said "let the little children come to me. Do not stop them; for the Kingdom of Heaven belongs to such as these." And so it does. Amen

Chapter 11

Happy Hour
in Hospice

*J*an was one of our nurses whom I had known for a long time. She was warm and loving with a great sense of humor.

She emailed me one day asking if I would help her pick out a prayer book. Her mother died recently and she wanted one like hers, but she did not know exactly which one it was.

I emailed her back with some ideas.

A few days later, Jan came in to see me and we talked about the prayer book, about her mother's death, and her brother's recent death as well. After she left, I knew something was not right about her.

A few months later, I heard that Jan was a patient on the fifth floor. I went up to see her, and after talking with family, I learned that she had developed a brain tumor. Our confused conversation from a few months ago finally made sense.

Jan was in and out of the hospital for a few months, enduring chemo, biopsies, and radiation, then a longer stay at a rehabilitation facility. Even though the doctors tried to shrink it, the tumor was inoperable. Those months were very difficult for Jan and her family. They grappled with Jan's diagnosis and tried to hang onto the hope that she would win the battle with cancer.

Jan and I had many conversations about this "invader" in her head. She called it "Herbie." We laughed about talking to Herbie and asking him to leave. She said that he would not talk to her. He was a silent killer.

Like every cancer patient, she wanted to fight, to give "Herbie" all she had to get rid of him. She fought as long and as hard as she could. One day, when she had come to terms with the fact that she was dying, she shared with me that Herbie finally spoke. He said to her, "It's going to be OK." She was at peace.

Throughout her final month, we talked about what she should do regarding her family, about plans if she didn't recover. With her family's help, Jan wrote up a living will and talked about her last wish, to go to the beach. The beach was her favorite place. I brought in a meditation CD with beautiful ocean sounds. We would spend a few quiet moments at the beach in meditation as often as we could.

Every year Jan and her family vacationed at the beach, where they had reservations for this coming July. It was only June. They hoped that she would be able to go one last time. Maybe she would rally just enough. It was not to be.

I continued to walk with Jan, helping whenever I could. I brought her medicinal aromatherapy essences and she loved them, especially Laurel Leaf and Douglas Fir. I put the drops on a gauze pad and safety pinned it to her hospital gown. Everyone knew when I had come to visit because the room smelled so wonderful. Jan referred to the essences as her "smelly stuff."

Jan was moved to the hospice unit a few weeks later. We were losing another staff member, a nurse who was so deeply loved and respected. She was too young. She was nearing the end of her life's journey, approaching her final door.

The end came slowly. Jan lingered for a few weeks. She became less and less responsive.

Towards the end, I went as often as I could to 'anoint' her with the aromatherapy essences. In addition to her favorites, I now added the ancient Biblical essences of Myrrh and Frankincense, the gifts that the Three Wise Men brought to the Baby Jesus. I also used Spikenard, the essence Mary Magdalene used to anoint the feet of Jesus shortly before His death. Fr. Joseph gave her Sacrament of the Sick. Fr. John and Fr. Joseph celebrated Mass in her room. We all prayed that she would go quickly and without suffering. There were many hugs, many tears, and lots of love.

Jan was surrounded by her family and bathed in love and light, when her door finally opened and she transitioned out of this life. It was July.

Jan never physically made it to the beach, but her family went in her honor. I am sure her spirit went with them, finally free.

Staring Death in the Face

What struck me most about Jan and her family was their courage to look at death and continue the rituals that held them together as a family: happy hour, laughter, the beach.

Through the years, Jan and her family enjoyed happy hour. Cancer didn't deter them from continuing this tradition.

Jan couldn't wait for happy hour to come. When she woke up every morning she would ask, "Is it 5 o'clock yet?" Her family would gather in her room in the late afternoon, paper cups in hand, and open a few bottles of wine, or beer, or whatever. Anyone who happened to be visiting at the time was invited to join in. I had the honor of raising my paper cup to toast Jan on several occasions.

During happy hour there were many laughs. Her friends and family recalled funny stories, touching moments, favorite places and people. Usually this happens at a person's wake when the bereaved family gathers. In Jan's case, her family and friends were able to remember these times with Jan herself.

I cannot even count how many people went in and out of her room every day. Family for sure, but so many colleagues: fellow nurses, doctors, friends, chaplains, priests. What a tribute to the many lives she touched. It was special and it honored a life well lived, but from our perspective, too short.

There were many tears when Jan died. We cried with relief that her suffering was over. We cried because we will miss her so much. We cried because our future together, once well planned, was changed forever without her.

Crying is so important in our lives. Our culture is so uncomfortable with crying, especially for men because it is considered "unmanly" and a sign of weakness. The same is true for helping professionals. My counseling professors warned, "Don't ever let them see you cry." It was considered a mark of vulnerability, not strength.

I am not afraid to cry with my patients, or let them see me cry. It is one of the most important expressions of feelings that we have as humans and it is a gift. I believe that if more people were encouraged and "allowed" to cry to let go of grief, anger, pain and suffering, our world would not be as violent. Sure, it hurts to cry, but releasing the tears can often lead to healing and wholeness.

My colleagues and I often talk about Jan, remembering fond memories and sharing funny stories. She is never far from our thoughts. Our love for each other is stronger than death. I feel her presence on

Sacred Heart 5 sometimes and when I walk the halls of the hospital, as she continues to bless us with her comfort, guidance, and healing.

Chapter 12

Butterflies

wice a year the Pastoral Care Department hosts a memorial service in our Chapel to re-member and honor those who have passed away at the hospital in the previous six months. We send out about 300 invitations to grieving families, and only about 100 people actually come. It is so hard to re-turn to the place where a loved one has died.

It is a challenge to write a reflection for these ser-vices that will bring comfort and affirmation to griev-ing families. I look for inspiration in many places, and I try to write what will bring comfort to me as well.

Below is a reflection that I wrote for our most re-cent memorial service.

"Butterflies. Monarch butterflies in particular. What an amazing creature! They grace us in the summer time with their elegant beauty, brightening our gardens and delighting our day. If we are lucky, we will catch a glimpse of the caterpillar, then the cocoon hanging on a branch, and finally the beautiful monarch.

Do you know that four generations of monarchs are born every summer? That fourth generation is born just before the fall. Then, as the cool weather comes and it becomes too cold for them here, the monarchs disappear. Just like that.

Where do they go? I used to think that they succumbed to the frost and freezing temperatures, but they don't. They fly 2,500 miles to the fir trees in western Mexico where they hibernate all winter. They arrive in Mexico on the same day every year, November 2, All Souls Day, Dia de los Muertos and return to the very same tree that their great-great-grandparents left the previous spring.

Thousands of them hang there on the branches, keeping each other warm, until the spring. Then, just before they leave the tree to begin their journey north again, they mate. They bring the new generation of monarchs with them, to be born here in our gardens in the spring. Amazing!

Now you may be wondering what butterflies have to do with our loved ones.

Like the monarch, our loved ones are with us for a time. They grace our lives, bring us joy, happiness and we love them. Then, like the butterflies, they are gone. They disappear from our sight. We are sad, thinking they are gone forever.

There is a scripture reading in the Gospel of John when Jesus talks about his impending death. His followers, his friends, are very troubled. Jesus tells them that he goes before them to prepare a place for them where he will be with them again. He tells them that they know the way there. His followers said, "How do we know the way, Lord?"

Maybe, like the butterflies, we know the way home. The butterflies instinctively know the way to Mexico, even though they were never there. They know exactly when to arrive each year. They are guided by a brain no bigger than the head of a pin. The Monarch butterfly makes the transition from egg, to caterpillar, to cocoon, to butterfly, all by instinct.

Our journey back home to heaven and to our loved ones is perhaps as strongly instinctual as the monarch's drive to journey to their winter home.

We sorely miss our loved ones, the hugs, the conversations, holidays and birthdays. It hurts, we grieve, we cry.

However, if we listen closely and look around us, we might receive some clues that they are still here, watching over us. A dream, a song, a whiff of perfume, a "feeling" we are not alone. They still love us, care for us. Love is the bond that transcends death. Death is an illusion, just a transition from flesh to spirit.

We are here on the earth with a mission, to love one another, to help one another, returning home when our earthly work is done. We reunite with our loved ones, and we know the way.

I'd like to share with you a beautiful reflection that sums up the message this evening. It's called "A Ship Sails."

A ship sails and I stand watching till she fades from the horizon. Someone at my side says "she is gone."

Gone where? Gone from my sight, that is all. She is just as large now as when I last saw her. Her diminished size and total loss from my sight is in me, not in her.

And just at that moment, when someone at my side says she is gone, there are others who are watching her come over their horizon and other voices take up the glad shout, "Here she comes!"

That is what dying is, a horizon and just the limit of our sight. (attributed to Henry Van Dyke)

Let us pray:

Lift us up Lord, that we may see farther. When the road we walk is dark, may we always hear the gentle singing of the birds. When times are hard may hardness never turn our hearts to stone. May we always remember that when shadows fall, we never walk alone. Amen."

Chapter 13

My Mother
Betty

The call came two days before Thanksgiving. I did not know at the time that this would be the call that I had dreaded receiving for a very long time.

I was in Maine, visiting my youngest daughter Amy. I was planning to stay another day to celebrate an early Thanksgiving because I had to work Thanksgiving Day.

The call was from my mom's nursing home. The nurse said that of all the urinary tract infections Mom had this year, this one was the worst. She also thought that Mom may have had a stroke. At 92 years old, this is really bad news. Could I come right away?

I was five hours away. I asked the nurses to continue to treat her and to ask the doctor to prescribe medication for her.

I collected myself, gave Amy a kiss, and headed back to Connecticut.

When I arrived at Mom's bedside, I was shocked. She couldn't feed herself, couldn't talk and couldn't get out of bed. I had dinner with her just a few nights before and she was fine. Was it a stroke or the symptoms of a urinary tract infection?

I eventually decided, with the nurses' help, to treat Mom in her room where she was comfortable. I didn't want to subject her to the trauma of going to the emergency room.

The doctor ordered intravenous antibiotics for three days, but there was no improvement. The doctor came to the nursing home to see her and I shared with him that Mom had a living will and didn't want any aggressive medical treatment done. She had been through so much already.

The day after Thanksgiving, I was at Mom's bedside, and the doctor called and asked to speak to me. He said that further tests were done and Mom's kidneys were failing. He recommended hospice.

My heart sank. Had the end really come? Mom was 92 and would be 93 in a few months. I saw the door. It loomed dark and threatening before us.

I always tell family members, even though you think you are ready for a loved one's death, you are never ready. I cared for my mom for the last eight years, and in many ways for the 45 years since my father died. I knew that this day would come. It was here but I was not ready.

As a chaplain, I walk through these doors with patients every day. When it is your own flesh and blood, it is quite another story. I was scared. I must go with her to the threshold and hold her hand.

I called my two brothers, and they agreed that hospice was the right thing to do because her kidneys had been compromised for some time. We surely did not want to see her suffer any more. So that evening,

I signed the papers to admit her to the hospice service. I was numb, and very sad.

Ever since Mom was in the nursing home we always planned a family Thanksgiving gathering with her there. This Thanksgiving was no different. We reserved the special dining room and everyone was coming. We did not expect that we would be saying our good-byes instead of celebrating. I called all the local family I could, and they came. It was touching, sweet, and sad. I felt like I was in a dream, a nightmare, really. I wanted to wake up. The door was looming larger.

I had to work the Monday and Tuesday after Thanksgiving, but in the afternoon I would sit at Mom's bedside. The hospice nurses were keeping her out of pain and comfortable, but she lingered. She slept, I cried.

Mom loved her classical music, especially opera. I kept the local classical music station playing those last few days so she could listen to her beloved music. In fact, a few years ago when we spoke about what she would like to have played at her funeral, she requested the last movement of Beethoven's Ninth Symphony, "Joyful, Joyful We Adore Thee" along with a few other favorite songs.

I arrived at about 2 p.m. on Tuesday afternoon, December 3, 2013, and my older daughter Jenny said she would come after work. Mom continued to sleep, she looked so peaceful. What was she waiting for?

When Jenny walked into the room around 5:30 p.m., Mom suddenly changed. Her breathing slowed and rattled, I had seen this many times and I knew it was close to the end. Jenny and I told Mom it was OK to go, that we loved her, that we would never forget her. I held her hand.

Mom always told me that she was afraid to die. I promised her that she would not be alone. I knew that her beloved Jesus would be there, and, as Mom planned it, my daughter and I were there, too.

Mom took her last breath at 6 p.m. as my daughter and I cried and cried. Then at 6:05 p.m., the radio caught my attention. Beethoven's Ninth Symphony began playing on the radio.

I sat in amazement as the hospice chaplain and the funeral home director arrived to take Mom. We all stayed until the Ninth Symphony ended with a flourish. Just like Mom, long Italian good-byes. Joyful, joyful! There are no coincidences in this world, only perfect synchronicity.

In her special way, Mom was telling me that she had safely walked through her door to the other side. She was the last one of her generation to cross over. No doubt all her sisters, brothers, my father, her dogs, her beloved cat Sheba, and her dear friends were with her too. The open arms of Jesus welcomed her into the Kingdom.

I emailed the radio station to share my mom's story with them. The host of the program was so very kind, and happy that he was the one who chose, unwittingly, to play Beethoven's Ninth that night. He said it was his favorite piece of music. I asked if he would play it again on her 93rd birthday, exactly eight weeks after she died. Even though he did not take requests, he did play the Ninth for my mom on her birthday.

There are many mysteries about the time of death. Sometimes loved ones wait for family members to leave the room before dying. Some wait for everyone to come before they die. Some die suddenly, leaving no time for family to prepare, to spare them a long, drawn out dying process. Some die on a special day, a holiday or birthday so that we will not forget them. I truly believe that these events happen with perfect timing and with love.

The loss of both parents marks the end of a generation. We are now orphans and we will be the next generation to cross over. Our own mortality is right in front of us. It can be terrifying. For me, the loss of my mom would send me into a tail spin that I couldn't see coming. Walking through the door of my grief was one of the hardest doors for me to enter.

My work as a chaplain continually reminds me that life is unpredictable and precious. The most challenging times can also be an opportunity to do and say the things that we have been putting off for a long time. Repairing relationships with an "I'm sorry", telling people we love them, and doing the things on our "bucket list" is so important.

The year following Mom's death would present me with opportunities to do just that, although in a way that I could have not imagined.

Chapter 14

Compassion
Fatigue

*I*t is the summer in the desert, the dark night of the soul.

On July 1, 2014, I left my position as Manager of Pastoral Care at Saint Mary's Hospital. I was planning to retire. I was a little too young, but it was a good excuse.

After the death of my mother on December 3, 2013, my visits to patients had become harder and harder. I would wince whenever the beeper went off, hoping the call was for a Bible or a prayer. I dreaded the call to the bedside of a dying patient.

My grief over my own loss was so great, I just could not be a chaplain to others anymore. I was exhausted.

There is a phenomenon in the helping professions called "compassion fatigue" or "burnout." It happens when chaplains, nurses or others in the health-care field, give and give of themselves and do not take time to recharge. Sometimes it comes on slowly, sometimes we can see it coming and take a leave of absence or extended time away from our work to recharge. Sometimes a brick wall comes up suddenly and we crash into it. The brick wall appeared after my mother's death, and I crashed into it, breaking into a million pieces.

I felt the call to the desert ever since my recent visit to Sedona, Arizona. The desolation of the desert was very inviting given my busy lifestyle. I made a plan. I would resign from the hospital, sell my house, and fill my car with a few things. I would drive to Sedona with my cat. I needed space to write, to meditate, to recover from grief and twelve years in the trenches of chaplaincy. I wanted a simpler life. I would have no job or place to live. God would provide the door to a new life.

I felt like I was following Jesus' example, going away for "forty days" in the desert to talk with God, to find myself again.

I put the house on the market and sold most of my furniture. I did all the right things. I staged the rooms, picked a starting price, and lowered it based on interest and viewings. Yet it still was not selling, not even one offer. The realtors were very surprised because it was a nice house in a nice location.

By now it was late fall. I began asking God what was going on. Was there a message here that I was not hearing? Where was the door to new life?

Given my plan, one might ask if I was running away from something. I knew I was grieving. I also knew that grieving people sometimes act irrationally. It's part of the grief process. I had seen it repeatedly in my patients and their families. I began thinking I was going crazy. Here I was, in an almost empty "staged model home" which was not selling, and with no job. What had I done?

We make plans and God gently laughs! Instead of travelling to the desert, the desert came to me.

I joined a grief group at my church. It was an intense group, meeting for a two hour session once a week for ten weeks. It became my oasis in my desert.

I entered the group thinking I probably would not get much out of it. I knew all about the stages of grief, the intense feelings, the need for time for healing and recovery. Maybe I could help someone else. I was wrong.

I needed to help myself. I began to realize that I was grieving many events in my life: leaving my job, my divorce 12 years earlier, grief from my father's passing 45 years ago, and of course, the most recent loss of my mother.

Everyone in the group listened as I poured out my heart. I listened to them as well. We all needed healing, a sacred space to talk where we were heard and loved, without judgment.

I needed to let go of many things: the grief, the need to control and the need to be needed. This was an exercise of taking care of myself, loving myself and accepting myself.

This is very hard to do for many caregivers. We are good at caring for others, but not ourselves. In my case, I think this is partly because I could not nor did not want to acknowledge the pain inside. It is very hard to stop, turn around, and say, "What are these feelings chasing me?" Once I identified the fear, sadness, and powerlessness, I could accept that they were in my life for a reason. They taught me acceptance, forgiveness and humility. They taught me to look at the past and avoid repeating it.

My breakthrough came unexpectedly. As I wrote in my journal, I remembered what happened after my father died on April 27, 1968.

Often grief does not really hit us until months after the death. A year after Dad's death, Mom remarried, sold the house and everything in it, and moved us all to London, Ontario, Canada, where she was raised and her new husband lived. My two brothers and I were not happy about this decision and we tried to get her to change her mind. This seemed like such a crazy idea, to pull us out of the home we grew up in and move away from all our friends. It was another loss on top of losing our dad. We were not successful in changing her mind. It was a disastrous year emotionally and financially.

Several months after we moved, it became clear to Mom that the marriage wasn't going to work. School had just begun and she didn't want to pull us out of school, although we would have been happy to go back anytime! We waited until the following summer and returned to Stamford, CT, to pick up the pieces and try to heal.

Was I repeating the past? Was I running away, just like Mom? Was I hoping if I changed my address these feeling would go away and I wouldn't have to deal with them?

"Wherever you go, there you are." This realization felt like a breakthrough. I *was* running away. Wherever I went, I would need to deal with the feelings of loss, fear, grief. It was as if God was saying, "Stop. Turn around. Feel the feelings. Release them and move on. Stay here with your family. They need you as much as you need them." I finally saw the door. It was right here.

With the help of the grief group, my family, as well as my Saint Mary's Hospital family, I was able to begin to heal.

Italy

About two months after Mom died, my brother Frank called me and said, "We have to go to Italy. Mom planned this trip from heaven!"

It was a cruise around Sicily for two weeks in October. The tour began in Sorrento on the mainland, where my father's mother was born and it stopped in Lipari, where my mom's grandfather was born. The cruise also stopped on the Island of Malta. My mom's brother was a Knight of Malta.

Could my brother be right, did Mom really plan this trip for us to help us heal?

I did not know at the time that this trip, which happened right in the middle of the grief group sessions, would be the key to my journey out of the desert.

I went to Italy. My brother and I visited all the places where our grandparents were born. In addition to the cruise around Sicily, we added a few days in Naples, where my grandfather was born. We hired a driver who took us to the Piazza Cappabianca and Via Cappabianca, outside of Naples. We enjoyed delicious Italian food that reminded us of our own family gatherings. We visited places where my grandparents walked, and basked in the same sun under which our grandparents lived. It was an amazing feeling, a feeling of being connected to all of them and being one big Italian family. I was reminded of my first mystical experience and the revelation that "we are one." We truly are.

We also found a distant relative, Pasquale Cappabianca, whom we met in Valletto on the Island of Malta. We shared family legends, and he knew some of the same stories that we heard as children about our family. Apparently, we were descended from monks or priests who wore "white capes", cappa (cape) bianca (white), whom Pasquale said were from an area in Tuscany where his family still owned vineyards. We sipped espresso in a beautiful outdoor modern piazza in the middle of the old city, the old and the new sharing the ground upon which many generations of many different cultures walked over the centuries. What an amazing meeting it was!

I met many wonderful people on the cruise. Some were also trying to connect with their family roots in Italy and Sicily, meeting up with distant relatives. Some were grieving the loss of a loved one. One woman had lost both her husband and son. Another was recently divorced, another had lost his wife from cancer. He decided to try to cope by taking a cruise every month!

I found I was able to listen to my fellow travelers with an open heart. I began to feel compassion. My pain was edging away just enough to let others in again. I felt like I was healing, the dark cloud of grief was beginning to lift. Light was beginning to stream through the door.

When my brother and I booked this trip so many months earlier, I had no idea how important it would be to my healing and my connecting to family. Sometimes a vacation is much more than a vacation. For me, it was a path to the next door of my life, my life without my mom.

I returned to the grief group refreshed and renewed and I had new light in me, a new purpose and a new understanding. I felt able to move on, slowly, but surely.

It was now November. The grief group ended and it was time to make some decisions.

I decided to take the house off the market and stay in Connecticut with my family. Sedona may need to wait for me for a time but I will be forever grateful that the desert door came to me right here where I was, when I needed it.

If I was going to stay in my home, I needed to get a job. Another door, another transition.

I really missed my Saint Mary's family so I kept in touch with many of them. I supported them over the years, and they supported me in my times of need. We cared deeply for one another.

One night, my dear friend Diane mentioned that there was an opening in the Gift Shop. No stress, just fun! I would be able to see all my friends again and feel at home.

That night when I logged on to the website to apply for the Gift Shop position, I noticed a posting for a per diem chaplain. It was just posted the day before.

When I left Saint Mary's I never thought I'd be a hospital chaplain again. I remember telling my grief group that the door to Saint Mary's was closed to me, but that God would open another door. Well, you can take the chaplain out of the hospital, but you can't take the chaplain out of the chaplain!

I questioned myself and asked God if I could return to chaplaincy. Was my grief and compassion fatigue healed enough so that I could support and care for patients and staff once again? Would I be welcomed back after leaving the hospital?

The answer was a resounding yes! I am happy to say that I have returned to Saint Mary's as a staff chaplain. Sometimes doors close only to open again when the time is right.

The homecoming was overwhelming! The first few months I received so many hugs and emails from staff who were really happy that I was back. I had no idea how much I was missed, and no idea how much I missed all of my colleagues. It has been a joyous reunion and an answer to prayer that I could never have imagined.

We make plans and God gently laughs!

Coming back to chaplaincy reinforced many things for me. There are no coincidences, only synchronicity. God's timing was perfect, both in the timing of the chaplain posting and in my stage of healing. I truly felt that I came back with a renewed sense of understanding. We all serve together at Saint Mary's with Divine Purpose, and we have a higher calling. We are doing God's healing work, by caring for each other and for our patients because God planned it that way. We are family. We are one.

I will be serving others with a renewed depth of understanding of the grief process and its complexities. I will also be more aware of the need to take care of myself. I am reminded of the flight attendant speech, "Put your own oxygen mask on before assisting others." I am not able to help others, or love others, unless I first take care of and love myself.

My journey in the desert began with the death of my mother. The journey ends with renewed life and finding my family roots in Italy and my spiritual home, Saint Mary's Hospital. I am humbled and grateful, and feel blessed by God for my chaplain ministry and for the grace and courage that He gave me to walk through the many doors to my new life.

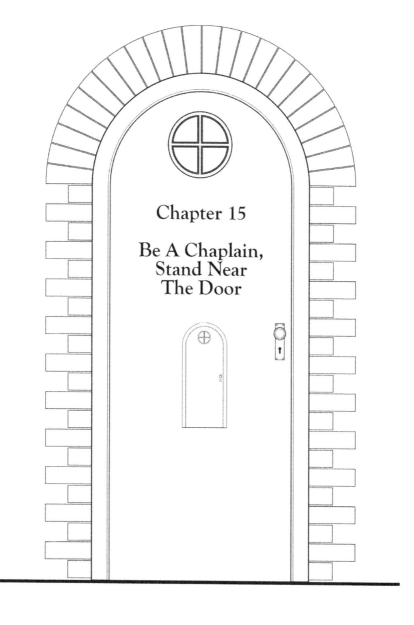

Chapter 15

Be A Chaplain,
Stand Near
The Door

e are nearing the end of our walk through the doors of the hospital. Thank you for walking with me, and I hope you have been as inspired as I was by these amazing souls and their stories.

I have learned so much from my patients whom I have helped, and who have helped me. All of us are on a spiritual journey together as we eternally transition through many doors. We are born and we die, surely, but our souls always journey toward God. If we ask our heavenly guides, our guardian angels, to guide us, we will receive the strength and courage we need to continue the journey, to walk through our doors. We help each other along the way, learning, growing in love and compassion, because love is all there is.

I will leave you with some insights to ponder, things that these amazing souls have taught me. These pearls of wisdom give me courage to walk through my doors. I pray that they will help you to walk through your doors as well.

- Life and death are mysterious and mystical. Embrace them. Don't be afraid to question your beliefs, to seek answers in unconventional places, to *change* because of new insights about yourself, God and the world.

- Do a life review. See the patterns and synchronicities in your life, even if some of them were challenging or downright terrible. See the love, the learning, and the blessings that are surely there. Then move ahead toward healing.
- Heal relationships. Identify regrets. Ask for and give forgiveness. It is never too late to say I love you or I'm sorry. If you can't find the person, or if they have died, write them a letter. Forgiveness is for *you*, not for them. Don't put it off, do it *now*. Then *move on.*
- If you are having trouble with grief or loss, talk with someone. A trusted friend, a chaplain or clergy person, or family member can walk with you through the difficult times. Find a bereavement group. Many hospitals, churches, and hospice organizations offer them. Open up, be vulnerable, be honest. The only way through grief is through it, not around it.
- None of us will get out of this life alive. Don't be afraid. Plan for your final days. Talk with family about your wishes. Talk with your parents about their wishes. Leaving this life peacefully, with dignity and respect is a beautiful tribute to a life well lived.

- Trust in God, whatever you perceive God to be. Pray, meditate and ask for guidance. Listen for the song of God in your heart. It is there in all of us, a precious gift, if only we will stop long enough to listen.

- Be a kind-hearted person. Live with gratitude in your heart for all the gifts of this life. Be generous of spirit. Be accepting of yourself and others, even the dark parts. The light in your heart will dispel the darkness without struggle.

- Be a chaplain. Look around at everyone in your life this day. Who needs someone to walk with them through one of their doors? Walk with them, listen to them, give a hug. Listening with your heart is the greatest gift you can give someone, and it doesn't cost a cent. It is priceless.

- Live in love, walk in love, and take care of each other. This is what chaplains do. Be a chaplain. Stand near the door for the one, or two, or three people whose hand you are intended to put on the latch of their door, and let them help you find yours.

- May God bless each and every one of you this day and in all the days of your life.

"Nothing else matters compared to helping them
find it,
And open it, and walk in, and find Him…
So I stand by the door"

I Stand by the Door
By Rev. Samuel Moor Shoemaker

I stand by the door.
I neither go too far in, nor stay too far out.
The door is the most important door in the world –
It is the door through which men walk when they
find God.
There is no use my going way inside and staying
there,
When so many are still outside and they, as much as
I,
Crave to know where the door is.
And all that so many ever find
Is only the wall where the door ought to be.
They creep along the wall like blind men,
With outstretched, groping hands,
Feeling for a door, knowing there must be a door,

Yet they never find it…
So I stand by the door.

The most tremendous thing in the world
Is for men to find that door – the door to God.
The most important thing that any man can do
Is to take hold of one of those blind, groping hands
And put it on the latch – the latch that only clicks
And opens to the man's own touch.

Men die outside that door, as starving beggars die
On cold nights in cruel cities in the dead of winter --
Die for want of what is within their grasp.
They live on the other side of it – live because they
have not found it.

Nothing else matters compared to helping them
find it,
And open it, and walk in, and find Him.
So I stand by the door.

Go in great saints, go all the way in –
Go way down into the cavernous cellars,
And way up into the spacious attics --
It is a vast, roomy house, this house where God is.
Go into the deepest of hidden casements,
Of withdrawal, of silence, of sainthood.

Some must inhabit those inner rooms
And know the depths and heights of God,
And call outside to the rest of us how wonderful it
is.
Sometimes I take a deeper look in.
Sometimes venture in a little farther,
But my place seems closer to the opening…
So I stand by the door.

There is another reason why I stand there.
Some people get part way in and become afraid
Lest God and the zeal of His house devour them;
For God is so very great and asks all of us.
And these people feel a cosmic claustrophobia,
And want to get out. 'Let me out!' they cry.
And the people way inside only terrify them more.
Somebody must be by the door to tell them that
they are spoiled
For the old life, they have seen too much:
One taste of God and nothing but God will do any
more.
Somebody must be watching for the frightened
Who seek to sneak out just where they came in,
To tell them how much better it is inside.

The people too far in do not see how near these are
To leaving – preoccupied with the wonder of it all.

Somebody must watch for those who have entered
the door,
But would like to run away. So for them, too,
I stand by the door.
I admire the people who go way in.
But I wish they would not forget how it was
Before they got in. Then they would be able to help
The people who have not yet even found the door.
Or the people who want to run away again from
God.
You can go in too deeply, and stay in too long,
And forget the people outside the door.
As for me, I shall take my old accustomed place,
Near enough to God to hear Him and know He is
there,
But not so far from men as not to hear them,
And remember they are there, too.
Where? Outside the door –
Thousands of them. Millions of them.
But – more important for me –
One of them, two of them, ten of them.
Whose hands I am intended to put on the latch.
So I shall stand by the door and wait
For those who seek it.
"I had rather be a door-keeper…"
So I stand by the door.

About the Author

Chaplain Geri is a spiritually inclusive, board certified chaplain, teacher, and friend. She lives in Connecticut with her rescue Siamese cat, Fia.

Geri welcomes your comments, stories and feedback. She is available for workshops and lectures. You can contact her via email at chaplaingeri@gmail.com, or through her Facebook page "Chaplain Geri Cappabianca."

Made in United States
North Haven, CT
16 March 2022

17211881R00095